MW00883729

Why GOD Thinks He Can Use YOU

GLENN HATCHER

As a missional thinker and practitioner, Glenn Hatcher has been developing Christian leaders and helping them to explore their place in God's story for over 35 years. Glenn and his wife Phyllis worked with emerging leaders on university campuses in America prior to spending 15 years living and equipping pacesetters in various parts of Africa, Russia, the Middle East and Europe. While still having a passion for cross-cultural ministry, the Hatchers returned to the United States in 2006 to develop and assist in new training initiatives for missionaries with Globe International. As well as a teacher and trainer, Glenn is a certified Christian leadership coach. Glenn and Phyllis have two adult children, and he enjoys good books, good music and good movies.

EIKON
PUBLISHING
For Life's Journey

www.eikonassociates.com
PO Box 3040, Pensacola,
FL 32516 USA

ISBN: 1439267758
ISBN-13: 9781439267752

ACKNOWLEDGEMENTS

This book is born out of my life journey and consequently has many unknowing contributors: friends who have sat and chatted over ideas and coffee from Georgia to Russia to Kenya to Morocco; acquaintances who have thought out loud in cloistered conversations; iconoclasts who have challenged me and pushed back with better ideas than mine. Most of these contributors don't know their impact. And some of them, I don't remember their names. But be they African or Arab, missionary, saint or sinner, they've made me think and pray and study. They've strengthened my faith.

But some people are known: my mom and dad, Jimmy Smith, Joe Glenn Smith, Bill Finke, L.A. Joiner in various and sundry ways have shaped my life, vision, values and ministry. They've instilled in me virtues and compassion and faith.

And my children, Zachary and Jane have grown up as unique world citizens watching my routines, listening to my stories, checking to see if my faith and rhetoric matched up to my daily life. They are breathing barometers, keeping me real.

I want to thank Phyllis for being the love of my life and the stalwart prayer champion all these years. She has been there through everything as a constant companion and abiding friend. She raised our children while I tramped the world, kept the home fires burning and called blind spots to my attention. But she has loved me without conditions and prodded me to love others the same way.

So, if I say anything good, it's probably because of all them. If I say anything wrong, it's my own fault.

Thanks.

TABLE OF CONTENTS

INTRODUCTION
(Read these bits first)

I've been a missionary in one way or another for more than 30 years.

For a decade, Phyllis and I raised both biological and spiritual children between the fraternity houses on a university campus while I traveled a circuit between three other smaller schools. Then, for 15 years we lived abroad and I traveled all over the world—from Siberia to Morocco, from Uganda to Belarus—teaching and training leaders, helping to develop churches (both underground in "creative access countries" and in free societies) and establishing Bible schools and training centers.

Consequently, I've studied the Bible. I'm really no expert; I'm just a learner. I've studied the Scriptures neither pedantically to accumulate titles, degrees and authority, nor in a proof-text manner to legitimize my lifestyle or to condemn others. But every day, for decades I've prayerfully poured over the Gospels, the Epistles and the Old Testament to find answers to the nagging questions of my heart. I love an unseen but genuinely present Jesus in an almost inexplicable way of commitment and passion after a mysterious college encounter with Him. I have studied the Scriptures as a way to know and follow Him.

My passion has been to make disciples and see churches grow. And pretty much, I've given my life for this.

When we returned to the United States after all these years to assist in developing the Globe International learning community, I was concerned that the things I had taught all over the world were being somewhat neglected in my homeland.

I'm writing this book because of my great burden for the church. It is my conviction that we are not what we are supposed to be. When we live sub-Christian lives, we thwart the great mission of God. The tension between what we know through tradition and culture and what is both taught and exampled in the Bible results in living below God's intention for us.

And because it is part of my journey of discovery, it has stories both personal and borrowed. My wife has given permission to talk about her and to pull back the curtain on her life as well as mine and of course, our life together.

The thesis of this book is that God finds us useful for His purposes because He invests Himself in us. His love is for everyone, but God invests Himself in those who follow Jesus in mysterious and genuine ways producing diversity for His purposes.

There seems to be confusion about what God expects of us and who does what. Or even if He thinks He can use us. The great gulf between clergy and laity leaves us with performers and spectators, suppliers and consumers. But that's not right!

If Jesus' life and ministry – and Paul the church planter's commentaries and directives – teach us anything, it's about a "flattening" of the church hierarchy and a releasing of the Holy Spirit. It's about empowering, not just in a general sense, but specifically for individuals and communities of Believers to do specific things. *This is the deep resonating sense of hope within men and women everywhere.*

I'm convinced that God calls every man, woman and child to Himself and accordingly equips and empowers them for His purpose and His pleasure. Since it's not all linear, predictable and rational, it is often messy and chaotic. But it is the interaction of a loving and graceful God that prepares us, equips us and makes us useful for Himself.

God thinks you are useful to Him. I want to tell you why.

Chapter 1

GOD IS ON A MISSION

The following dialogue is a prison scene between Andy (Tim Robbins) and Red (Morgan Freeman), excerpted from the movie *The Shawshank Redemption*. Andy has just served 2 weeks in solitary confinement for playing an operatic aria over the PA system. Now he enters the dining hall, where curious inmates await him.

HEYWOOD
Couldn't play somethin' good, huh?
Hank Williams?

ANDY
They broke the door down before I
could take requests.

FLOYD
Was it worth two weeks in the hole?

ANDY
Easiest time I ever did.

HEYWOOD
*… No such thing as easy time in
the hole. A week seems like a year.*

ANDY
*I had Mr. Mozart to keep me company.
Hardly felt the time at all.*

RED
*Oh, they let you tote that record
player down there, huh? I could'a
swore they confiscated that stuff.*

ANDY
*(taps his heart, his head)
The music was here…and here.
That's the one thing they can't
confiscate, not ever. That's the
beauty of it. Haven't you ever felt
that way about music, Red?*

RED
*Played a mean harmonica as a younger
man. Lost my taste for it. Didn't
make much sense on the inside.*

ANDY
*Here's where it makes most sense.
We need it so we don't forget.*

RED
Forget?

ANDY
*That there are things in this world
not carved out of gray stone. That
there's a small place inside of us
they can never lock away, and that
place is called hope.*

RED
*Hope is a dangerous thing. Drive a
man insane. It's got no place here.
Better get used to the idea.*

[Fast-forward to scene 38—Andy has escaped from prison and Red has been paroled and is reading a letter from Andy.]

RED
(**reading**) *Remember Red, Hope is a
good thing; maybe the best of
things. And no good thing ever
dies.*

(taken from The Shawshank Redemption, scene 20. Written by Frank Darabont.)

⌘   ⌘   ⌘

Hope.

Hope!

Red says a mouthful when he says, "Hope is a dangerous thing." Alexander Pope nailed it when he said, "Hope springs eternal in the human breast."

Hope is dangerous *and* eternal. Hope is that deep thing in us that expects more, and expects it with passionate desire. Hope is that human quality without which we really cannot exist.

The nature of man is to yearn for something better. That's hope. If you say, "satisfaction guaranteed," look out, because you are in for trouble because dissatisfaction is tied to unfulfilled hope. And the nature of man is to never be satisfied, but to passionately hope for something more. The nature of man is to yearn for something better: an adventure to live, a mountain to climb, a race to run, a world to conquer.

I love how T.E. Lawrence (known better as Lawrence of Arabia) puts it: *"All men dream: but not equally. Those who dream by night in the dusty recesses of their minds awake in the day to find that it was vanity; but the dreamers of day are dangerous men, for they may act their dreams with open eyes, to make it possible."*

That's hope – open-eyed dreams.

THE LONGING FOR A BETTER WORLD

Since you're holding this book, it is likely that you have a deep desire to be used of God. You sense and know that things are not as they should be. The world is not the way it's supposed to be. You just know it. There is a longing deep within for answers to the dissonance in society; the lack of purpose and vision that keeps us grounded and moving forward.

To be human is to hope. Vacav Havel, the brilliant and thoughtful former president of the Czech Republic in his book

Disturbing the Peace says that hope is "an orientation of the spirit, an orientation of the heart; it transcends the world that is immediately experienced, and is anchored somewhere beyond its horizons... Hope is definitely not the same thing as optimism. It is not the conviction that something will turn out well, but the certainty that something makes sense, regardless of how it turns out."[1]

The world around us has a longing for something more. You can hear it in their songs. Turn on the radio, almost any station. You'll hear them. Love songs. They cry out for a perfect world; they cry out for a perfect love and the perfect relationship between a man and a woman. They express a longing for total commitment, total transparency, unconditional love, honor and respect.

Read a book. Watch a movie. And understand that there is a cry for something more. That cry comes from a hope deep within— a hope that somehow all will be righted and things will be good.

Humans long to be part of the solution.

The great desire for super heroic intervention is everywhere! From comic books to TV shows to movies to video games— people want to see justice prevail. And people seem to know instinctively that justice will only triumph and that things will only be righted when common everyday people are endowed with supernatural strength and power!

Even kids know this. Give a little boy the choice of pajamas to buy and he'll come up with Spiderman or Superman or some

---

1   *Disturbing the Peace* (New York: Vintage Books, 1990, p 181)

other hero who can fly or spin webs, beat up bad guys, defend and rescue. At the least, it will be a cartoon character that wins the race and beats the bad guy. Give him a stick and it will become a gun or a sword to defend his castle or free his maiden.

This is a longing for spiritual strength. With a few exceptions, men, women, even children seem born with a desire to be a change-agent for good and to make the world a better place. And there is a deep hope that somehow it will happen in spite of all the difficulties and frailties of human life. Mankind seems wired for that optimism and hope. But mankind is frustrated. Instinctively the world knows that things are wrong, and people want to see the wrongs made right. We want results. But the great hope that is within mankind remains a dream—a dream that it would take something truly supernatural to make it happen.

Wouldn't it be great for someone to make it all happen—to fix it, to heal it! Deep down inside we know it must be possible. And those who have discovered the reality of God's story even want to be part of the cure. There is a pervasive cry for superhuman abilities to arise thwarting injustice, liberating the abused and marginalized and making things the way they *should* be.

In our hope, we sense something about God.

WE LONG FOR A GOD WHO IS GOOD

Seemingly every culture recognizes an ultimate "God" of some sort—some kind of Supreme Being. Perhaps it's because it is human to desire to experience supernatural transcendence and

His wisdom. As Christians, we want to experience God's love and His mercy and His compassion—the attributes we read of in Scripture. And we want God to be good and just and merciful, and strong, and involved in the lives of people. He can't be a wimp and He can't be absent or passive. God *has* to be good and involved.

And our longing for God is sometimes entwined with disappointment, manifesting too often in our "we-don't-understand" questions: "Why would God allow this? Why doesn't God do something? If He's good and just, why does He allow these things to happen and persist?"

Sometimes when we ask these kinds of questions, we forget that all of the goodness we would attribute to our seemingly absent God has been embodied in a tangible form we can actually understand: Jesus. He is the fullness of the Godhead, in human form. He was, and is, good and just and kind. He healed the sick, gave sight to blind eyes, everywhere He went. He died both because He did these things and because He wanted these things done; and not just in a dusty little corner of Palestine, but everywhere.

The hope that resonates in every heart of every person on the planet is actualized in Jesus Christ. He is everything that everyone has hoped for. And His love is available to every person

> **"What comes to mind when we think about God is the most important thing about us."**
> **— A. W. Tozer**

on the planet who would like to sense His peace, goodness and love in their lives.

The death of Jesus is a fact. He died because of evil, but He died also to defeat evil. He died because of injustice but also to produce justice. He died because men are selfish and arrogant. Jesus died because of evil but also because of good.

But He didn't stay dead!

He was resurrected by an awesome God to actualize hope in a dying world and every Believer gets to be a part of that Hope!

And again, this is where you come in. You, as a follower of Jesus, have this actualized Hope living in your own soul! Christ lives in us.

God wants to use us as we learn how to manifest to others those attributes of goodness and love, and faith to heal!

WHAT IS GOD ACTUALLY AFTER IN THE WORLD TODAY?

There is a Divine reason for your existence. It began at Creation. God had an idea for mankind, and it's been playing out for millennia. Along the way, people have ignored Him; disobeyed Him; forgotten how to know Him. This mess-up has necessitated a few changes in plan, perhaps. But it should comfort you to know that He is not standing in the heavens with a lightning bolt for a spear, ready to judge and destroy His creation and those who fail to repent.

This has been a popular notion for the last hundred years. But what if there is more to what God is doing in the earth than that? God has a much different plan for us. Putting it simply, He plans to fix everything.

Anglican Bishop N.T. Wright, in his many poignant writings, says over and over that God's mission is to "put everything to rights."

God is on a mission! And that mission would restore creation – and us as creatures within it – to right relationship with the Creator God. The results would be that all of creation would reflect who God is.

And that's where YOU come in!

Yes, YOU are one of those whom God has chosen to "do good" in this hurting world. There is no one quite like you. No person on earth has YOUR particular frame of reference; YOUR upbringing; YOUR set of challenges—and victories. You are unique in the entire world. And God can use YOU like He can use no other.

God intends to use His people – the church – in His mission. The fact is, God wants to use everyone, all the time, everywhere to advance His kingdom and to do good.

OUR MISCONCEPTIONS OF GOD

The problem is, we're still having a hard time conceiving of a God who is interactive and intimate.

Sometimes we think of God as The Grand Watchmaker in the sky. We've been taught this in our religious and academic world. We get this idea that the God of creation made a mechanistic world something akin to a big watch. He wound it up, said, "That's good," and then stepped back allowing creation to run on its own, refusing to interfere. And by doing this, we basically reject the supernatural reality of God. He made it all, but he's not active in His creation. The Watchmaker view allows us to have correct religious beliefs, but they are based on human reason and observed features of a rational, understandable world. Basically, we think if we can get enough facts, assemble enough data and think it through scientifically, we can figure it all out. After all it's based on evidence, logic, laws and principles. Or is it?

Or maybe we think of God sort of like a stage Magician, sort of a grand David Copperfield, who shows up occasionally, does a few tricks, a few miracles, and then moves on. We're always looking for the next show. We're waiting for when and where The Magician will show up. (Maybe He'll saw a woman in half this time!) The Magician has more involvement in creation than the Watchmaker, but He's not really active in the world. Not really. He's active some places and sometimes. But not everywhere. Not all the time.

Or maybe we see God as the Grand Puppeteer running everything with strings attached. He makes it all happen, manipulating people unsuspectingly. He is involved but yet manipulative in His involvement. He moves people irresistibly, making them do what He wants. His pleasure is working the strings.

Don't believe any of it! God is active in His creation, not passive. He's active even among those who deny His existence. He's active among those who are running from Him. He's not the disaffected Watchmaker watching from a distance. He's not the occasional trick Magician, showing up once in a while to dazzle us with His tricks. Neither is He the Puppet Master pulling all the strings, making sure that everything is done as He decides.

God is active in His creation, calling people to Himself.

While we were living in Cyprus, a young Pakistani man came to my office. He explained that he was a student in the university and had been in Nicosia for over a year. As he sat on the sofa opposite my desk, he nervously fidgeted with the baseball cap in his hands. He kept his eyes on the floor as he talked. "Every night I have a dream of a tall man in a white robe. He stands before me and I can never see His face, only that He wears a very bright white robe. And He speaks to me in a gentle voice and every night He says, 'Follow me'." Raising his eyes he looked unblinkingly at me, "You don't have to tell me who He is. I know He is Jesus. What am I to do?"

A young Iraqi student came to our home and told me of a similar recurring dream of the man in the white robe. When he told his mother about this man in white, she began to weep. "You know," she explained to him, "I had this same dream before you were born. Over and over He came to me asking me to follow him. But I never knew how." She immediately began working to get her son out of his home country and out of the family home fearing that should he become a follower of Jesus, the family would kill him. He stood in my living room and explained the mystery of his dream and how he was looking for a way to follow Jesus.

A friend of mine who does research for a large denomination tells me that these are not isolated experiences. He estimates that annually there are over 100,000 Muslims who have similar experiences of either dreams or visions of a man in white who asks them to follow him. Or sometimes it's the angel Gabriel who says, "Follow Jesus." This propels them on a five to seven year journey to find out what it means to follow Jesus.

While training a group of young leaders in the underground church of a North African country, I asked them how many had comparable experiences of a supernatural encounter with Jesus. Of the almost thirty former Muslims who were gathered in this mountain retreat, the majority told of experiences of dreams and visions calling them to Jesus. For them their first encounter with God had been a totally non-church, out-of-the-box experience.

God is active in His creation. He is the unseen God active in all events and lives in the earth. He's the One who is closer than our breath. He is always revealing Himself and He has made us His co-laborers.

WORKERS WITH GOD

God uses people. Amazing as that might be, the Creator God of the universe uses committed people in a partnership with Himself.

One of my favorite Bible stories happens in the book of Acts. It involves angels and non-believers who have visions and church leaders that struggle and food and paradigm shifts. This story shows us how God works in human lives while revealing our part in His plan.

The story begins by telling us about a guy named Cornelius. He is a not a Jew, but an outsider who as a Roman soldier is stationed with his family in Palestine. He commands many men and is prominent in the community. He regularly prays to the God he doesn't know. He is devout, generous and God-fearing. He cares about God—whom he does not really know—and about people.

One day he has a vision and sees an angel who addresses him by name and informs him that his prayers have been heard, and that God has seen how he has given to the poor. Then the angel instructs Cornelius to send men 30 miles south to Joppa to bring back Simon Peter, a follower of

> **The fact is, God wants to use everyone all the time everywhere to advance His Kingdom and to do good.**

Jesus who obviously has a message for him.

Peter is in the midst of his own faith crisis at the seaside home of Simon the Tanner in Joppa. He's wrestling with the whole paradigm shift that Jesus, His life, death and resurrection has produced.

Jesus has made God more accessible than before. Through His life and teachings, then through His death, burial, resurrection and ascension, Jesus has changed everything about how people relate to God. Following Pentecost, where the Holy Spirit is poured out on and into the Jesus-followers, God no longer confines Himself and His activity to a particular group of people (Jews) in a particular place (Jerusalem) who keep special laws (Torah) and lives a special way.

God is loose in the earth!

Although Peter was involved in this whole movement, chapter 10 of the Book of Acts shows us that he was still somewhat confused and reluctant to implement all that he understands.

As a good Jew (one of God's insiders), Simon Peter doesn't associate with non-Jews. He doesn't eat non-kosher; he doesn't go to non-Jewish homes, neither does he eat with those who do not keep his customs. And he's troubled by a trance-like vision he has experienced. While in this trance, a large sheet is let down like a giant picnic cloth. Strange enough, but the big problem is that it is populated by all kinds of "unclean," non-kosher animals. The voice of the vision says, "Get up Peter, kill and eat."

Peter is repulsed and protests this temptation, "I've never eaten anything impure or unclean!" But the voice says, "Do not call anything impure that God has made clean."

Three times this happens. Three times! And then the Holy Spirit says to him, "Three men are downstairs looking for you. Get up, go downstairs and don't hesitate to go with them, because I've sent them."

Peter accompanies these men to the home of Cornelius (albeit still somewhat reluctantly), explains the Good news of Jesus and the Holy Spirit fills them all, even though they were not "insiders." They were Gentiles. Non-Jews.

Here we see the way God works to accomplish His mission in the earth. God is at work in the lives of unbelievers and believers as well. God is on a mission!

God does supernatural interventions like sending angels and giving dreams and visions to men and women like Cornelius. But then He requires men and women, like Simon Peter, to interpret these dreams, angelic visitations and explain about Jesus as workers together with God.

As co-workers with God, He does His part and we do ours (see 1 Corinthians 3:9). It is the supernatural, interactive and intimate God who touches lives and dispatches angels and gives dreams and visions. We can't do this, but He can. Our part is to be present in all parts of the world, expressing His attributes in our own tangible lives. Each of us has a story to tell that gives explanation to His supernatural dealings. We are the storytellers who explain what God is doing and participate with him in the establishment and expansion of His kingdom.

HOPE OF GLORY

One of the major themes of Scripture concerns God's *glory.* What is God's glory? In the Old Testament, the Hebrew word *kaboud* is translated "glory." This carries with it the idea of the "weight" of God. God's "presence" is "weighty."

In the New Testament, the word used for "glory" is the Greek word *doxa.* And this word basically means, "to reflect."

Remember at the birth of Jesus when the angels appeared to the shepherds? Luke 2:9 says, *"...the glory of the Lord shone round about, and they were sore afraid."* The glory of the Lord was that sense of His presence manifested as bright light and heaviness, that sense of His presence that engendered fear among the shepherds. At that moment, somehow there was a reflection of who God is in holiness, in righteousness. As the One who is "completely other;" not like us, completely different.

But glory is also the idea of reflecting who God is in character, presence, love, gentleness, mercy and grace. These are things *we* can reflect! The idea of glorifying God is the idea of living our life in such a way that people see the attitudes and attributes of the eternal God in us. It *is* possible!

God has crowned humans with glory. God has crowned men and women with the ability to reflect everything that God Himself is. In Psalm 8, the psalmist cries out to God,

Oh Lord, our Lord, How majestic is Your name in all the earth! You have set Your glory above the heavens. Out of the mouths of babes

and infants, You have established strength because of Your foes, to still the enemy and the avenger. When I look at Your heavens, the work of Your fingers, the moon and the stars, which You have set in place, what is man that You are mindful of him, and the Son of Man that you care for him? Yet You have made him a little lower than the heavenly beings—even God himself!—and crowned him with glory and honor.
(Vss. 1-5)

Throughout the Scriptures, we are told the purpose and plan of God is that all the earth be filled with His glory. This means that all the earth is to be filled with the men and women who exemplify the robust nature of God.

> **There is a cry for superhuman abilities that thwart injustice, liberate the abused and the marginalized and make things the way they should be.**

This is God's dream! This is God's desire! And instinctively, we as human beings know it because of that deep-seated, super-hero desire to make things right and have justice prevail!

We also are aware that we have fallen short of reflecting who Jesus is, and who God is. We are painfully aware that somehow, we have exchanged the ability to glorify God for our own independence.

Yet in spite of our failures, our conflicts and our frailties there remains this deep sense that even if things are not right there is a hope that they can and should be made right. Regardless of situations, we sense deep inside that things shifting toward "rightness" are somehow possible.

In the letter to the Ephesians, Paul, the church planter, refers to a "glorious church," or a church filled with God's glory. Paul is not referring to a building, of course. Paul is referring to a people, the people of God who by their actions, by their attitudes and by their motives reflect the nature of God.

In Psalm 72:19, the psalmist cries out, *"Blessed be God's glorious name forever; May the whole earth be filled with His glory!"*

The idea is that the whole world—the whole universe—would reflect the nature of God.

It is this "hope of glory." That resonates in the heart of men and women everywhere.

JESUS IS GOD

God wants all of His creation to reflect who and what He is: to reflect His character, His holiness, His power, His love, His mercy and justice.

And Jesus did that.

When Jesus came into the world, He came on a mission. It wasn't happenstance or accident that Jesus was born, that He led a life of teaching and making disciples, doing miracles and touching lives. It wasn't a misfortune that Jesus was killed. It was a plan. It was part of God's mission. He had to die in order to be resurrected.

Jesus came with a mission. Jesus came with the purpose.

Jesus came to show us what God the Father is really like. And to redeem a creation that had gone wrong. Jesus said, *"If you have seen me, you have seen the Father"* (John 14:9). Jesus reflected, who God the Father truly is.

There always seems to be a controversy and question surrounding Jesus' divinity. As He walked the earth, was He actually God? Was He a man who became God, or was He in fact God who became man?

In many ways, these are almost childish questions because what we really know about God is what we see in Jesus. Jesus reveals the Father embodying His love, kindness and power. Jesus said, "If you've really seen me you've seen the Father. If you see me you know what the Father is like." He implies that His life, His mercy, His grace is a one-to-one correspondence with that of the Father.

Jesus shows us what the Father is like. Jesus engenders the totality of God's love. And we see it in Him, and want to emulate it.

Jesus came to destroy the works of the enemy. Jesus came so that the negative, deadly, caustic works of the enemy could be reversed. That justice could be seen in the earth; that mercy could be seen among people. Jesus came with a mission to bring redemption to God's creation and bring reconciliation to God, to creation and one another.

Jesus' death, burial and resurrection began the work. Jesus' redemptive work—that which He began on the cross and completed at the Ascension and Pentecost—cannot be repeated. These are "once and for all" acts that only He could perform. Yet the Good News of His redemptive acts needed to be conveyed throughout the earth.

JESUS CALLS HIS CHURCH TO MISSION

He left this unfinished mission to be completed by His people: the church. He began the work, and God placed all things under His rule and appointed Him to be head over everything for the church, which is His body, the fullness of Him who fills everything in every way.

As Jesus departed (in His super-heroic nonconventional way—through the clouds) He said to His disciples, "All authority and weight in heaven and on earth has been given to me. Therefore, go and make disciples of all families of people, baptizing them in the name of the Father and of the Son and of the Holy Spirit, and teaching them to obey everything I have commanded you. And surely I am with you always, to the very end of the age" (Matthew 28:20).

The point of being human—made in God's image—is to reflect God's stewardship of love into the world in ways of redemption and transformation.

Missio Dei

Jesus said He personally would build His church. He is referring not to an institution or a building or a program but a people. The church is a people from diverse backgrounds with a new identity, a new purpose and a new power through the abiding presence of the Holy Spirit.

The church is the sent people of God. They are the ones involved in the *"missio dei"*—the mission of God. *Missio dei* is a Latin theological term that can be translated as "the sending of God." We are on a mis-

> *All we really know about God is what we see in Jesus.*

sion with God. We are a missional people. The *missio dei* is God's unfolding story from Genesis to now, and into the future. The *missio dei* is God's intent to fill the earth with His glory. It is God's mission to establish His Kingdom—that space where what God wants done is actually done—in the earth.

For some, it is a surprise that there are actual places in the universe where what God wants to happen does not actually happen. And it may challenge your theology, but the truth remains that there are places where *what God wants done is not actually done.*

Someone asked the question, "Are you telling me God is not sovereign?" But sovereignty is not about God having His will carried out. Sovereignty is about God being able to make His own choices within Himself. God is sovereign; He doesn't have to consult anybody about anything. But Jesus taught us to pray, "Thy kingdom come, Thy will be done on earth as it is in heaven." That prayer would indicate that what is happening on earth is not necessarily all that God wants done.

A baby may die of malnutrition in the shadow of a church building. That is not God's will. People die because they have bad drinking water. That is not God's will. Evil reigns and teenage girls are unwillingly sold into prostitution. That is not God's will!

The kingdom of God is that space where what God wants done is actually done. And Jesus has conferred on His disciples a kingdom. We are ambassadors of the very kingdom of God and we have been given the message of the gospel—the Good News of that kingdom—to take to all peoples of the earth.

Jesus died so that the kingdom of God could be established in the earth–God's reign in the earth.

Jesus was sent by God in the power of the Holy Spirit. Jesus has sent the Holy Spirit to us His people. Jesus has instructed us to incarnate—to live out in our daily lives—the Good News of God's kingdom.

The church is God's idea for redemption through reflection. When the church displays God's character, God's nature, and God's life—in real-life situations—redemption happens! When the church sees itself as a sent people of God carrying His message and living His life, transformation happens in the lives of individuals, in families, in communities—in the lives of whole people groups!

When the church fails to live out what God sends them to do, redemption slows down. The purposes of God are thwarted. And God is mocked.

Mahatma Gandhi, the great Indian leader, admired Jesus and often quoted from the Sermon on the Mount. Once when the missionary E. Stanley Jones met with Gandhi, he asked him, "Mr. Gandhi, though you quote the words of Christ often, why is it that you appear to so adamantly reject becoming His follower?"

Gandhi replied, "Oh, I don't reject your Christ. I love your Christ. I do not like your Christians. Your Christians are so unlike your Christ."

And we could be very offended at Mr. Gandhi. We could be upset that he could say that about us. We could, if deep inside we didn't know that what he says is true. It seems that the world has no real problem with Jesus,

> **The Kingdom of God is that space where what God wants done is actually done.**

it has a real problem with the us—His people. And actually we know that we have problems. We are often judgmental, arrogant, self-righteous and prejudiced.

Hey, you know it's true!

Oftentimes this is the problem we find, we as God's people—the church—often conduct ourselves not in ways that glorify (reflect) Christ, but in ways that bring Him shame.

God's intent was and is that the church—those who believe in and follow Christ—would represent Him to the extent that we would manifest the very wisdom of God on earth. By so doing, we would make His goodness known to the angelic and demonic rulers and authorities in the spiritual realm, where ideas live and breed; even where societal bents and public policies are conceived. And by *being* what we believe, we should literally change society.

The church is a people formed by God for Himself from every family of people on the earth for His purposes with a common understanding, common goals, a common vision and a common responsibility to reflect all that He is, and to take His grace and goodness to the most remote corners of the earth. The church has a common proclamation that "Jesus is Lord" and a common identity found in the indwelling Holy Spirit.

Christopher Wright, in his book *The Mission of God,* says, "...It is not so much that the church has a mission but that God's mission is the church." It is the heart cry of God that none should perish, but that all should come to repentance. Each one who repents becomes part of the church and by the very nature of that membership should have compassion to win others as well.

It is the intention of God to display His nature, His character, His power, grace and love in and through His people, the church throughout all generations, forever and ever! It just doesn't stop but gets bigger and better until everyone everywhere is involved. The mission is completed when the whole earth is filled with His redeemed people reflecting who He is!

CHAPTER 2

GOD IS UP TO SOMETHING

"*Folks, the world knows what this {the church} is supposed to look like. Years ago in New York City, I got into a taxicab with an Iranian taxi driver, who could hardly speak English. I tried to explain to him where I wanted to go, and as he was pulling His car out of the parking place, he almost got hit by a van that on its side had a sign reading "The Pentecostal Church." He got real upset and said, 'That guy's drunk.' I said, 'No, he's a Pentecostal; drunk in the spirit, maybe, but not with wine.'*

"*He asked, 'Do you know about church?' I said, 'Well, I know a little bit about it; what do you know?' It was a long trip from one end of Manhattan to the other and all the way down He told me one horror story after another that he'd heard about the church. He knew about the pastor that ran off with the choirmaster's wife, the couple that had burned the church down and collected the insurance—every horrible thing you could imagine.*

"We finally get to where we were going, I paid him, and as we're standing there on the landing I gave him an extra-large tip. He got a suspicious look in His eyes—he'd been around, you know. I said, 'Answer me this one question...' (Now keep in mind, I'm planning on witnessing to him) 'If there was a God and He had a church, what would it be like?'

"He sat there for awhile making up His mind to play or not. Finally He sighed and said, 'Well, if there was a God and He had a church—they would care for the poor, heal the sick, and they wouldn't charge you money to teach you the Book.'

"I turned around and it was like an explosion in my chest. 'Oh, God!' I just cried, I couldn't help it. I thought, 'Oh Lord, they know. The world knows what it's supposed to be like. The only ones that don't know are the church.'"

– John Wimber, founder of the Vineyard Church Movement

⌘   ⌘   ⌘

YOU ARE USEFUL TO GOD!

What a statement! What a possibility!

There are many amazing and sometimes conflicting thoughts that enter our minds when we think about ourselves being useful to God. And I mean the BIG GOD: the Creator of the heaven and earth; the Eternal One who made it all and keeps it all together.

Perhaps you begin by thinking: **Why?** Why would this God ever want to use me?

It's like watching one of the commercials on TV where an off-camera voice says something to the guy on-camera. He stops, looks at the camera, touches His chest and says, *"You talking to me?"* (Sometimes, with an attitude; sometimes not. Depending on what they're trying to sell.) I mean why would God actually want to use me, of all people? Why would a God who knows everything, who knows the end from the beginning, who has all power and all knowledge really want to use me? I mean, if He actually made everything in six days, just by speaking, why would He want to use me? Can't He just say it and make it happen?

And then there is: *How?* How could He ever use me? I mean, I can understand Billy Graham and Mother Teresa and people like that. I mean even Bono—I can understand God using him. But me, how could *I* possibly be useful to God?

But then maybe you could begin thinking: *What if?* What if God really did want to use me? What if His intention has always been to use everyone, everywhere, all the time–to use them as change agents in a world needing change? What if I were to find out how I can be useful to Him, in the way He wants?

What if in God's heart of hearts, He wants something different from the way things are? What if the status quo is not the way things were meant to be? What if the deep longing of my own heart to make a difference, to be a superhero with powers for good able to stop divorce and poverty and hunger and AIDS is really real? What if this is really what God wants, too? And what if He wants to use me to achieve it?

The big question of God's people—whether living in the Old Testament or as Jesus-followers today—is how to live out their identity as a called and sent people of God living in the created world, filled with crisis and chaos.

The fact is, God wants to use everybody, everywhere all the time to advance His kingdom and to do good! That's what this book is about: the awesome reality that God wants to use you.

To understand something of God's plan, we need to unpack three Bible words: *love, grace and usefulness.*

GOD'S LOVE

We can never say enough about God's Love. But perhaps we can say too much, especially without saying anything.

God's Love is unconditional and universal.

God loves everyone—the whole world—every person whether good or evil, whether church-going or church-despising, whether chaste or promiscuous, drunk or sober, loving and kind or conniving and vengeful. God loves Hindus and Muslims, Christians and Jews. God loves homosexuals and homophobes.

And God's love carries no conditions. You cannot earn His love—you can't do enough or be good enough. And you cannot cause Him to stop loving. You can't be bad enough or callous enough to stop Him loving. God loves because He *is* love. Love is His nature. He loves from His being. It is His quality of existence to love, without condition, without even having the objects of His love returning that love.

God just loves. God loves because He is. (There you go—a good existential statement, and yet a mystical statement, as well, because it is somehow beyond our understanding and reasoning.) It's a mystery!

And we really need to understand—as best we can—the profound mystery that God loves everybody all the time.

I recently heard someone painfully say that they understood Christianity like this: *God is good; I am not; Try harder.* What a burden to bear! What a task to attempt: becoming good enough to be accepted and loved by a good God. It genuinely pains me that someone carries that level of misunderstanding. But it was both a taught and learned concept. It has no "grace" only "works" and blocks all understanding of God's unconditional love.

God is good. His goodness is expressed in His passionate and unfailing love. We must get past the issue of either being worthy of His love (because no one really is) or working to receive His love (because no one really can work enough or has to).

God loves His creation and us as His creatures, because He is the very essence of love. Everything about him is motivated by love. His love is pure. His love is just.

Of course we do have to be careful that we don't cheapen God's love by saying its universal. The fact that something is universal does not make it inexpensive. God shows His love by loving us when we actually had no use for Him. God demonstrates His love by sending His son, Jesus into the world to redeem the world through His life and death and burial and resurrection.

God loves everyone, regardless of his circumstances or station in life. His redemptive love extends to everyone. There is nothing anyone can do to provoke God to stop loving.

REALITY CHECK

Our world teaches us much about how to look at ourselves. It teaches us how to judge ourselves, and our successes. "Self image" is the way we see ourselves while "self esteem" is the way we feel about what we see. And those feelings pretty much determine our lives.

The way we see ourselves is determined by so many factors and filters: how we grew up, parental relationships, family security, ethnicity, etc. We don't have time to explore all these, but mostly we judge ourselves according to the way we see ourselves, and what we expect from ourselves.

In our heads, we have a story that plays over and over again. It defines who we are, and shapes how we feel about ourselves. In this story, we measure our success by the way we feel about ourselves and the apparent outcome of our endeavors in the acceptance we feel from those around us. And from God.

If self image is how we see ourselves, self-esteem is how we feel about what we see. Issues of self esteem flow from that story in our head. That story either affirms us or condemns us. It shapes us, and often alters the dreams of our heart—those dreams of a better world, those dreams of being who we want to be, those dreams of making a difference.

Sometimes we measure our success by an equation like this:

SUCCESS EQUALS PERFORMANCE DIVIDED BY EXPECTATIONS.

If we start out with high expectations (which we all do), but perform badly our sense of success is very low. We didn't "cut it," we didn't "make it," we "blew it" and we feel bad about ourselves.

Feeling this way usually leaves us with three alternatives:

- Increase performance (production)—do more so that we can feel better...
- lower our expectations—decide to expect less from life, ministry, people and God
- do away with the equation

In a performance-driven world, sometimes we are forced to measure our spirituality by religious works. Church attendance, Bible reading and religious activities are used as internal measuring sticks of our true commitment and true spirituality. When the expectations are set high—either by the program-driven church culture, parental or situational expectations or by the story in our head (or a collusion of them all)—we find it hard to measure-up. So we try harder to "up" our performance. We get up earlier, sing louder, attend more meetings, watch more Christian television or chase the newest Christian fad or church fancy. We "up" our performance. We work harder to feel successful and perhaps to feel a greater sense of God's love.

But we usually fail after a short time. How much more can we actually do to meet our own expectations, or the expectations of those around us?

On the other hand, we can just lower our expectations. We can never actually do it right, so why try so hard? We can lower our values of Scripture—*It's just words written by men thousands of years ago.* Or the church—*They're just a bunch of hypocrites who sit and judge others.* Or the Gospel—*There are many roads to God; this whole exclusive Jesus thing is overrated, bloody and antiquated.* And even God himself—*If He's actually out there He doesn't care about me.* Lower the expectations and we don't have to reach very far to be "spiritual" in our own eyes.

When Phyllis and I first got married (a long time ago), one day she said to me, *"I've taught myself not to expect very much so that way I'm never disappointed."* I just stared at her thinking maybe that's why she'd married me! I was the result of her low expectations! But I said, *"That's not very Christian is it? Isn't faith about always expecting more than we can actually produce or*

make happen? And we actually run the great risk of being either dis-
appointed or succeeding don't we?"

We can up our production. We can lower expectations.
Or we can do away with the whole equation and somehow look
at success from God's point of view.

WHAT ABOUT GOD'S PERSPECTIVE?

Success from God's perspective is obedience that comes from
faith, birthed through an intimate personal relationship with
Him.

The love of God is evidenced to us through the grace of God
in objective acts through Christ Jesus and the Holy Spirit. God
acts in time and space in His creation. He acted in the past
when He sent His son Jesus as an act of His love, as a means
of His grace. And when we respond in faith to these objective
acts—the birth, the life, the death, the burial, the resurrection,
the ascension and the sending of the Holy Spirit—things happen inside of us to alter the story in our head and reactivate the
dreams of our heart.

Turning from our old ways and putting faith in what Jesus
did produces in us a release from guilt found in our past actions,
motivations, attitudes, failures and what we have experienced.
Faith in Jesus' sacrifice and the amazing ramifications releases
us from the guilt of what we have caused in others. Sure we've
done wrong. We've not lived up to the standards others have
set for us. We've not even lived up to the standards we've set

for ourselves. We've injured others, we have done things we shouldn't and not done things that we should. And we feel guilty—mainly because we are guilty.

Faith in Jesus releases us from guilt, and we begin to experience His love. We move from the nebulous bumper-sticker flippancy of "smile, God loves you" to a deep internal understanding of His deep passionate love for us.

Faith in what Jesus accomplished releases us from fear of the future and what might happen. Faith in Jesus the Messiah, establishes our place in His *future*. Who He is and what He desires to accomplish becomes for us a motivation for doing righteousness.

> **Success from God's perspective is obedience that comes from faith, birthed through an intimate personal relationship with Him.**

Faith in Jesus' objective acts releases us from the grip of the present world system and all that is happening around us.

This results in several things. One of these is *moral authority*. Moral authority is the ability to stand righteous in the face of trial. Moral authority resonates in our super-hero longings and gives us the ability to say no to temptations and fears. A compassionate moral standard and a true moral authority sit squarely in our hearts as bedrock for our faith. We can say no to failure easier and yes to goodness easier because we are not burdened down with guilt.

Secondly, faith in Jesus' acts gives us a set of _transcendent values_. By this I mean, who I am and what I value depends on God and who He is and what He values. His values are different and relational rather than based on performance and works. God values a gentle and quiet spirit; _"...the hidden man of the heart, in that which is not corruptible, even the ornament of a meek and quiet spirit, which is in the sight of God of great price"_ (1 Peter 3:4). God values meekness and joy. God values peace and those who seek it.

When we value what Jesus values, we are motivated to be different and to act differently toward others.

Faith in Jesus' completed works gives us a _counter-culture mentality_. Although we are in the world system, we are not part of it. Our motivations are different. Our love is different. Our understanding of performance and success is different.

A sense rises up in us—that although things are not right, we can make them right, or at least be a part of the rightness. We understand that we are not just here, stuck in the moment, but we're part of a movement of change that endures and touches lives.

Because of our faith in Jesus and His acts of obedience, we experience _covenant relationships_ through the church—that community of love and forgiveness; that safe place of trust and of mutual acceptance. In finding people of a consistent passion to live out Jesus' teachings together, we find security and hope. Seeing God's love demonstrated through a mutually forgiving and encouraging community of people shape how we feel about God, how we feel about ourselves and how we conceive God's redemptive mission.

THE POWER OF THE CHURCH

There is wonderful diversity in God's covenant people. The differences of people, languages and cultures are enhanced and appreciated in the church. They form a rich tapestry of beauty in the sight of God because He has loved them and transformed them.

When two or more of these gather together, that is a church meeting. When believing men and women come together, the dynamic of their coming together is amplified by the assured presence of the risen Christ in their midst by the Holy Spirit. He has promised to be among us when we gather. *"For where two or three are gathered together in My name, there am I in the midst of them."* (Matthew 18:20)

The church is worldwide. In almost every nation of the earth, there are Believers. There are those who believe in the Lord Jesus Christ and trust Him in faith for their lives. In some places, Believers meet openly and bravely. They proffer political solutions and social remedies. But in some places believing in Jesus and offering one's life to Him endangers one's life. Believers do not enjoy the same benefits, yet they are endowed with the same Savior and Lord. Disenfranchised and marginalized by the majority, they suffer persecution and sometimes fear. Yet their faith grows along with their sense of purpose.

God is up to something in the world today. He is bringing us together, so that He can send us out.

> *To love means loving the unlovable. To forgive means pardoning the unpardonable. Faith means believing the unbelievable. Hope means hoping when everything seems hopeless.*
> *— G. K. Chesterton*

Our message is not just about some event in the future, a "catching-away" or heaven when you die. A steady diet of those kinds of messages leaves the church impotent and nearsighted. Instead of being empowered by a deep understanding of God's love and forgiveness to live fruitful lives *here and now*, it can leave God's people metaphorically standing at a bus stop dreamily awaiting the coming bus that will take them to some happy land.

This mentality keeps us spiritually bankrupt in the present, reaching awkwardly for some future reward. As the unconditionally loved followers of Christ, we have riches in the here and now, riches that are not of this world. Further, we have the ability to bring good news of *present* peace and joy to a beleaguered generation!

All the talk about God's love could possibly lead to nothing but a deep subjectivism and an abnormal desire for touchy-feely experiences. But if we honestly know God's love and realize that His love has for Himself resulted in action, we are spurred toward action in ourselves.

So how does this unconditional and universal love of God work in real life?

CHAPTER 3

THE GRACE-FAITH
CONTINUUM

*E*rnest Hemingway, in his short story The Capital of the World, digresses to the story of a father and his estranged son, Paco. The son had wronged his father and in his dishonor ran away from home. The father searched all over Spain for him, but could not find him. Finally, in the city of Madrid, in a last desperate attempt to find his son, the father placed an ad in the daily newspaper. The ad read: "PACO MEET AT HOTEL MONTANA NOON TUESDAY ALL IS FORGIVEN, PAPA."

The father prayed that maybe the boy would see the ad and maybe—just maybe—he would come to the Hotel Montana.

And on Tuesday at noon, the father arrived at the Hotel Montana. He could not believe his eyes! A squadron of police officers had been called out to keep order among the eight hundred young boys named "Paco" who had come to meet their father in front of the Hotel Montana. Eight hundred boys named Paco read the ad in the newspaper and hoped it was for them.

⌘ ⌘ ⌘

GOD'S GRACE

Unlike God's love, God's Grace is both conditional and specific. Grace is what God does for us that we cannot do for ourselves. Grace is God's transfer of favor on us for specific purposes that God Himself knows.

Often when we use the word "grace," we seem to say that it's God looking the other way when we do wrong. Somehow we see "grace" as God letting us off the hook for what we have done, or some sort of "pre-forgiven state" so that we can continue to live our lives in the way we want without consequence or penalty.

Someone once told me that there are three ways God deals with things: *justice, mercy and grace*. Justice is *getting what you deserve*. Mercy is ***not** getting what you deserve* (when you deserve the worst); and *grace is **getting what you do not deserve*** (when you deserve the worst).

THE GRACE OF RESCUE

We could say there are many ways of looking at grace in the Bible. Mostly, we are familiar with what I term, the "Grace of Rescue." This is that wonderful favor that comes from God when we do not expect it and certainly do not deserve it. It's that Grace of Rescue that brings reconciliation to God.

There is a great sense that things have gone so wrong and that evil is so prevalent that we desperately need someone to save us and rescue us from the world around us. And this is the cornerstone of the Christian story. This is the Grace of Rescue. It is God's grace, restoring us to right relationship to God Himself. It is the Grace of Rescue that grabs us and frees us from the slavery of our lusts, our egocentricity, our pettiness and small thinking and frees us to dream and explore the deepest longings of our heart.

I find that these passages written by Paul to one of His disciples named Titus explains grace in an amazing way:

It wasn't so long ago that we ourselves were stupid and stubborn, dupes of sin, ordered every which way by our glands, going around with a chip on our shoulder, hated and hating back. But when God, our kind and loving Savior God, stepped in, He saved us from all that. It was all His doing; we had nothing to do with it. He gave us a good bath, and we came out of it new people, washed inside and out by the Holy Spirit. Our Savior Jesus poured out new life so generously. God's gift has restored our relationship with Him and given us back our lives. And there's more life to come—an eternity of life! You can count on this.

–Titus 3:4-7 (The Message)

The Grace of Rescue is about God showing us specifically His love and mercy. It's about our reception by God into His family. That's the grace that rescues us.

One of the definitions for the Greek word that we translate "grace" is "that which causes pleasure." Grace is "… that which bestows or occasions, pleasure, delight or causes favorable regard."

Paul the church-planter writes to one of his groups of believers and says: *"God raised us up with Christ and seated us with Him in the heavenly realms in Christ Jesus, in order that in the coming ages He might show the incomparable riches of His grace, expressed in His kindness to us in Christ Jesus. For it is by grace you have been saved, through faith—and this not from yourselves, it is the gift of God—not by works, so that no one can boast,"* (Ephesians 2:6-9 NIV).

God's love, reaching out to us extends a grace of rescue.

The Grace of Identity

A sound biblical experience of grace also restores and reinforces our identity. As we better comprehend God's grace, we more clearly know who we are and how we see and feel about ourselves.

Paul writes to the Jesus-followers in Corinth, and says: *"… by the grace of God I am what I am, and His grace to me was not without effect. No, I worked harder than all of them—yet not I, but the grace of God that was with me,"* (1 Corinthians 15:10).

Grace comes with the encounter with God and gives us a taste of what can be. We often call these *dreams*. These are those deep seated sense of purpose, plan and disposition that causes both immediate dissatisfaction, but ultimately hope and passion.

Paul sees the grace that comes from God working in him in such a way that it gives him identity. He finds His identity in God's grace. When Paul says, "I am what I am by the grace of God," he is referring to how the grace—that undeserved favor of God—works in his life and through his life.

The natural (yet supernatural) response to grace is faith. Grace is God's extending Himself to us. Faith—actually believing what He has done—is our response to Him and His grace. When God gives grace, we respond and receive it by faith.

As we receive God's grace by faith, it changes us and molds us. It softens the hard places in us, and makes us strong where we are weak. It is God's pleasure working in us that re-molds our character, re-casts our visions and awakens our dreams.

When we rely on God's grace for our identity rather than what others say about us (whether good or bad!) or the story in our head (we talked about that in the last chapter), we see things from a different perspective. We become what we are by relying on God's goodness expressed in His unearned favor and pleasure to us.

When Paul says, "I am what I am by the grace of God," it is Paul's reliance on God's great work of redemption and transformation in his life giving him identity. No longer does his

identity come from his race, heritage, sexual orientation or religious rigor and duty. Paul found His identity in his grace-
filled relationship with the risen Jesus.

Understanding "who we are" helps us envision our place in
God's plan of redemption and move beyond being spectators to
active participants. Knowing "who we are" moves us to a place of
anticipation and action. We become aware that God wants to use
us, and to work together with us to bring change to our world.
We begin to see how our lives are being changed and we are more
and more being made to reflect God's character, love and mercy.

The goal of being a disciple of Jesus and responding to His
grace moves us into an intimacy with God. We ask the question "Who is God?" and we get an answer. We get a better
understanding of our personal spiritual identity. We can ask
"Who am I?" and through His grace have a better sense of self-
worth. And we get a real vision and hope for personal ministry.
We can ask "What will I do with my life?" and receive a sense
of destiny and direction.

THE GRACE THAT EQUIPS AND EMPOWERS

Somewhere along the way, I came across this:

To run and work the Law commands
Yet gives me neither feet nor hands;
But better news the Gospel brings:
It bids me fly, and gives me wings.

The gospel is about grace—God's sovereign choice and giving His favor. The gospel is not just about trying harder and failing. The Christian story is not "God is good; you are not; try harder"—even though you do get that sometimes from religious people.

And grace is not just about coming to Christ, receiving forgiveness and saying no to the world. It's much more. Grace encompasses God's work of empowering and equipping us for usefulness in His purpose and plan to redeem all creation and advance His Kingdom. Grace is about empowering us to run the race and complete the journey victoriously and with intention.

While God's love is universal—He loves everyone equally—and unconditional since it is His nature to love, God's grace is very particular and conditional. We must receive grace by faith. God's grace is conditional. Even though it might be extended because of God's loving nature, it is received by faith.

Grace is particular—in that it is given out in the Body of Christ as Christ Himself distributes it. In his instruction to the church in Ephesus, Paul reminds them that *"...to each one of us grace has been given as Christ apportioned it."* (Ephesians 4:7) Grace is given without strings attached.

Living in East Africa for a number of years we were faced with a communication problem when the word "grace" was linked to the word "free." The Kiswahili word for "free" is the word *"bure"* which is often translated as "worthless." *Free equaled worthless.* When we think in terms of grace being free, that does not mean that it is without worth. True grace is expensive, costing God a great deal, even the brutal death of His Son, Jesus.

God gives precise measures of specific grace to equip and empower us for our part in His Story. Grace is given purposely through God's choice to fulfill the purposes of life. The response to grace is always faith. Or should always be faith.

USEFULNESS TO GOD

Usefulness from God's perspective is obedience by faith through an intimate relationship with Him.

The premise of this book is to explore why God in His infinite mercy and goodness wants to use you to accomplish His purposes in the earth. It is about how He has equipped you, empowered you and is teaching you so that you might be part of His Great Mission to change the world.

It was Mahatma Gandhi who first said, "Be the change you want to see in the world."

Frankly, most people never know that they are useful to God. Many good church-going people have a sense that God only uses big-name people to do big ticket things with mind-blowing results. Somehow many people have the idea that God only uses the elite to move mountains, reshape the course of rivers and be Mother Teresa. They are unaware that usefulness from God's perspective is simple obedience to the tasks that we learn through an intimate relationship with Him.

As I set aside time to do this book, I was asked what it would be about. I replied, "It's about how God wants to use everybody all the time everywhere to advance His kingdom and do good." The sweet, amazingly helpful young lady who had asked the question just stared at me and blinked. It was obvious that she had never considered herself in any way useful to God. Sad.

GOD'S STORY

God's story is unfolding and we are to be a part of it. It is a story of salvation. It is a story of redemption.

Somehow over the last few decades we have been robbed of "story." The Gospel has somehow been reduced and married to a marketing strategy.

Robbed of story, we are a generation who has lost a sense of mystery. It seems, as my Scottish friend would say, that we have "lost the plot." And in losing the plot, the Gospel becomes more about avoiding hell and somehow making it into heaven. We've developed presentations with an ease of communication that become bumper stickers, Four Spiritual Laws and the Roman Road. In our quest to give certainty and to develop memorable formulas somehow we have lost connection with the "big story" of God.

And humans need a great story to fit ourselves into. We need something heroic. We need purpose and meaning. That deep sense that we are significant to God and that our actual living should bring change and improvement in our world continues to cry out!

> **Because we have been denied "the story," we have also been denied "the mission" as well.**

Because we have been denied "the story," we have also been denied "the mission." Wrong thinking about the kingdom of God has set us on a course of competing agendas where our methods are in conflict with our values, where our lifestyle is not consistent with our message.

We invite people into "a personal relationship with Jesus" using a bullhorn, standing on a platform, developing no sense of relationship with the people we address. Relationship is more than that.

Somehow, we have divided conversion from discipleship. We have found discipleship to be time-intensive and that in itself is a problem. We have been robbed of moral transformation because our story doesn't ring true in our lives and in the lives of the people with whom we share it.

Becoming a Christian means that we embrace the story and become part of it. Without a sense of story there is little compelling about Christianity. It seems to have no passion.

It seems to have no creativity. It seems in the eyes of many that Christianity lacks vibrancy.

⌘　⌘　⌘

"It is hard to be brave," said Piglet, sniffing slightly, "when you're only a Very Small Animal."

Rabbit, who had begun to write busily, looked up and said: "It is because you are a very small animal that you will be Useful in the adventure before us."

– A.A. Milne, *Winnie the Pooh*, 1926; p.94

CHAPTER 4

GOD CALLS...

G od calls every man and woman not just the elite. God calls us back to His original intention for our lives. God calls us back to our part in His Story.

COMMAND AND PRIVILEGE

The call of God is both a command and a privilege. It is a command because God expects us to respond. It is a privilege, because we are able to respond to God.

When Jane my daughter was small, we lived in a house with a porch swing—one of those big old Southern swings. It was one of our favorite places to be together. Often as Jane played nearby, I would call her and say, "Jane, come here." In calling Jane, it was both a command and a privilege. It was a command, because I wanted her to come and sit with me. I would not have called her if I had not wanted her to respond. But it was a privilege, because she got to come and sit on daddy's lap, and no one else got to sit on daddy's lap.

A call from God is a call for obedience. When God calls us back to Him it requires us to respond. We have to leave what we are doing, put aside those things that occupy our time and fill our hands and come to Him. It's not about excuse-making or delay. When He calls us it is so we will come.

My mentor and hero Jimmy Smith says, "The call of God is always 'Come here!'" It is always a call to further intimacy and instruction from the Father.

Paul writes: *I urge you to live a life worthy of the calling you have received. Be completely humble and gentle; be patient, bearing with one another in love. Make every effort to keep the unity of the Spirit through the bond of peace* (Ephesians 4:3). It is a reminder that in living out the command and privilege of God's call we should live humbly and gently. The privilege of the call should not go to our head but should be worked out in forbearance, love and unity.

So He calls us unto Himself, and back to the original purpose that He had for our lives. No matter how old we are or how young, no matter how many mistakes we've made or successes we've had, God calls us unto Himself that we might live out His purposes for us.

In American English, we most often talk about our "vocation" as our job—that thing we do to earn a living in order to educate our children and put food on the table. But actually the word "vocation" comes from the Latin word that means "to summon" or "to call." The root of the word comes from the idea of something "vocal"—something spoken.

In God's economy, "vocation" does not equal "job." The "vocation" we have is the calling of God. The "job" we have is the laboratory where we work out and carry out our vocation.

Ephesians 2:8-10 (The Message)

Now God has us where He wants us, with all the time in this world and the next to shower grace and kindness upon us in Christ Jesus.

Saving is all His idea, and all His work. All we do is trust Him enough to let Him do it. It's God's gift from start to finish! We don't play the major role. If we did, we'd probably go around bragging that we'd done the whole thing! No, we neither make nor save ourselves. God does both the making and saving.

He creates each of us by Christ Jesus to join him in the work He does, the good work He has gotten ready for us to do, work we had better be doing.

THE CALL TO BE

God calls us back to His original intention for our lives. God calls us back to our part in His Story, to be who we were always intended to be.

There is no wall between what's holy and what's not. God calls us to Himself and to become life-long apprentices to Jesus.

God has always had a plan for us. He has always wanted us to be part of His solution. Part of His redemption plan. When we basically had no use for God, and did not understand the yearning of our heart to make things right, we were still included in God's plan.

Although our parents may have told us that we were mistakes and unplanned (smile), God never saw anyone that way. Every child born into the world has a plan and a purpose from God. Whether they're born on the streets of Calcutta, the mountains of Appalachia, or the penthouses of New York City, every child has a destiny.

THE CALL TO DO

As we become who God wants us to be, we begin to do what God wants us to do.

Destiny is a non-transferable assignment from God. Destiny refers to something given by God to be accomplished by the individual in his lifetime. Destiny is not something forced upon you in some predetermined fashion, but an invitation— a call—from a loving God to a life-time assignment. We are called to be part of the task force to remodel and reshape the world according to the pattern of Jesus.

Paul, the church-planter, writes to the Jesus-followers at Ephesus, "For by grace you have been saved through faith. And this is not your own doing; it is the gift of God, not a result of works, so that no one may boast. For we are His workmanship, created in Christ Jesus for good works, which God prepared beforehand, that we should walk in them.

Here, Paul is emphasizing that salvation is a matter of grace. It's not a matter of doing good works. It's a matter of grace. It's God doing for us what we could not and cannot do for ourselves. We cannot work enough to experience God's salvation. It is a gift of grace.

And of course our response to this grace is faith. (Faith is always the correct response to grace! Didn't I say that already?) Faith reaches out to receive what is given by grace. That which is given by grace and received by faith cannot be boasted about or held onto as something "worked for."

Works God Has Prepared

We cannot be saved, changed or transformed by works, but we are saved to do works. In verse 10, Paul states that we are God's workmanship, created in Christ Jesus to do good works. In the Greek Paul uses the word *poema* which is translated "workmanship." From the word *poema* we get the word "poem." We are God's poetry. We are His workmanship, His creation, and we are created to do good works.

And it appears that those good works are prepared beforehand. They are our destiny. They are our assignment from God that cannot be transferred or given to another. They are given to us to walk out in our lifetime. As we discovered them and walk them out in our daily lives, we reflect God's glory.

God calls us unto Himself and asks us to live a life worthy of that calling. For those who love Him and have yielded to His calling and His purpose, He works everything in their lives to bring about "good" from His perspective (Romans 8:28).

But the call of God is not back to nostalgia. Not back to what could have been. God calls us forward and He sends us forward with His purpose.

God calls us unto himself and into a relationship of fellowship with His Son Jesus Christ. Fellowship with Jesus is an amazing thing. The fact that we can have fellowship—true *koinonia,* a Greek word from which we get English words like communion and communication—is one of the great mysteries of the ages. It is a spiritual reality that we have fellowship with Christ; that He speaks to us and that we learn from Him. In that fellowship, there's a genuine intimacy and that is a great mystery.

THE CALL TO RELATIONAL SUPREMACY

As we respond in faith, the relationship with Jesus becomes the primary relationship of our life. All other relationships are secondary to our relationship with Christ and they flow out of ours with Him.

They have to. Jesus is so specific about this that it's scary. He says, *"If anyone comes to Me and does not hate his father and mother, his wife and children, his brothers and sisters—yes, even his own life—he cannot be My disciple,"* (Luke 14:26).

Many cannot understand or accept the word "hate" here. And I hesitate to attempt to water it down by saying something stupid like, *"What Jesus was trying to say here?"* Jesus didn't <u>*try to say anything.*</u> He pretty much just said it. Right?

Jesus is talking about a call to relational supremacy in following Him. If the relationship with father and mother, spouse or children interferes with following Him into the world and into your destiny, you should leave them behind. *This is not about divorce or child abandonment!* But it is about having an intimacy and passion for the calling and sending of God that challenges your comfort, personal status quo and cultural norms.

> "What is the most important social relationship in your life? What place, what group of people do you feel dependent upon for survival? It is usually something associated with economic livelihood, personal advancement, or social influence..."

And the call to follow Jesus is about self-denial. We hear much more about "self-fulfillment" than we do "self-denial." In a world that invites us to instant total self-gratification, pleasure and fun, the idea of cross-bearing and denial of our wants and desires seems antiquated.

"If in fact most Christians are more rooted in the principalities and powers of this world than they are in the local community of faith, it is no wonder the church is in trouble. Clearly, the social reality in which we feel most rooted will be the one that will most determine our values, our priorities, and the way we live. It is not enough to talk of Christian fellowship while our security is based elsewhere. We will continue to conform to the values and institutions of our society as long as our people's security is grounded in them."

(— Jim Wallis, *The Call to Conversion* p.117)

But again, Jesus was very specific: *"If anyone would come after Me, he must deny himself and take up his cross daily and follow Me. For whoever wants to save his life will lose it, but whoever loses his life for Me will save it. What good is it for a man to gain the whole world, and yet lose or forfeit his very self?"* (Luke 9:23-25)

But when we begin to compare the adventure of living out our day-to-day God-assignment in His Story or looking after one's own interests, self gratification, welfare and personal advantage, where is the comparison? The choice between being a change-agent, answering that deep heart-dream that the Father has placed in us, and doing anything else seems ludicrous.

To make any comparison between the joys of knowing you are doing what you were created and redeemed to do, and anything else—no matter how rich and pleasurable it is—is just a joke!

Over half a century ago, C. S. Lewis put it this way:

"If there lurks in most modern minds the notion that to desire our own good and earnestly to hope for the enjoyment of it is a bad thing, I submit that this notion has crept in from Kant and the Stoics and is no part of the Christian faith. Indeed, if we consider the unblushing promises of reward and the staggering nature of the rewards promised in the Gospels, it would seem that our Lord finds our desire not too strong, but too weak. We are half-hearted creatures, fooling around with drink and sex and ambition when infinite joy is offered to us, like an ignorant child who wants to go on making mud pies in a slum because he can't imagine what is meant by the offer of a holiday by the sea. We are far too easily pleased."[2]

Here's where it gets sticky: Everybody has a destiny to live out, a ministry of service and a lifetime to please God—it is their vocation—and we have a specific environment in which to fulfill it. Some get to do it in "ministry" by standing before people and preaching. Some get to cross cultural barriers and live in places where they are the minority race, culture. Some get to work in their hometown in banks and hospitals

2   C.S. Lewis, *The Weight of Glory*, pp 3–4

and cabinet shops serving their employers and fellow employees. But all are called and sent.

GOD GATHERS TO SEND AND SENDS TO GATHER

The Call of God is both a command and a privilege. It is both general and specific.

God calls us unto Himself so that He might send us to the world because God is a sending God.

Jesus said to His disciples, *"...As the Father has sent me, I am sending you,"* (John 20:21). Jesus was sent by God in the power of the Holy Spirit. Jesus has sent the Holy Spirit to us His people. Jesus has said to us to incarnate—live out in our daily lives—the Good News of God's kingdom.

Responding to God's call means we respond to His Mission. We are the sent people of God. We are the ones involved in the *"missio dei"*—the sending of God. We are on a mission with Him. We are a missional people. The *missio dei* is God's unfolding story and we are part of it. The *missio dei* is God's intent to fill the earth with His glory.

Living missionally shifts our spirituality from passively waiting for evacuation to active involvement and participation in God's work of bringing reconciliation and restoration. The love and purpose of God becomes our motivation. We become agents of His grace, His love and the power of His life everywhere, all the time. Every situation is an opportunity to bring redemption, healing, and wholeness.

But God did not stop with just calling us to Himself. He did not stop with just giving us assignments. God in His mercy, grace and wisdom has also equipped us with a means of carrying out His Mission.

How Can I Actually Know the Calling of God in My Life?

Here are some ways to clarify and better understand God's calling on your life:

- Pray specifically asking God to tell you His plan and listen for the voice of God.
- Check the deep heart "impression" of what you believe God wants you to do.
- Watch for unexpected opportunities that come your way.
- Be sensitive to an extraordinary touch from God.
- Be careful of "pigeon holes" and labels like "I'm a prophet!" "I'm a pastor!" "I'm a prayer warrior!" Callings usually develop over time through intimacy with the Father.

> **Destiny is a non-transferable assignment from God.**

- Avoid ruts and routines. Look for what God is doing and saying to you personally.
- Listen to your heart and know your true passions.
- Think in terms of sacrifice and costs. Ministry always comes at a price. God always calls us to follow Him with sacrifice. If there is no sacrifice, I doubt it is either a call or true ministry.
- Avoid over spiritualizing your call. Few of us have "Damascus Road" experiences like Paul.
- Listen to those who know you best, who can be objective. Sometimes we need a "strategic outsider" to help us see ourselves.

CHAPTER 5

GOD GIFTS ACCORDING TO HIS CALL...

When Phyllis and I were first married, I made a big mistake. Now, I've made a lot of mistakes since then, but not this same one. And this particular mistake had to do with a fundamental understanding about the nature of "gifts." So, here's what happened...

Phyllis and I had been married for a short time and there arose an occasion for gift-giving. I can't remember whether it was a birthday or our first anniversary. But I surveyed our house (which didn't take long since it was tiny!) looking for something that Phyllis *needed* so I could give it to her as a gift. And I decided that she *needed* a cake plate—one of those footed things with a glass cover. Perhaps a wee bit unromantic, but I figured every woman *needs* a cake plate, right? And in my great wisdom, understanding and enthusiasm, I went to the store and bought one, had it wrapped and brought it home for the festive gift-giving occasion.

There was lots of hoopla and anticipation about the gift in the big box. After all, we were newlyweds and everything was exciting, new and mysterious! I waited anxiously for the moment when she ripped off the paper, opened the box and looked inside to find a token of my great love. Meanwhile, Phyllis, like any young bride, probably envisioned something more chic and more romantic!

We agree that a gift is something voluntarily transferred by one person to another without compensation. Here is the problem: some people see gift-giving as expressions of love and exercises in light-hearted frivolity, while others view gift-giving as a love-act that *meets a need* reinforcing and assisting in functionality. Function versus frivolity. Merriment versus meaning. Purpose versus pleasure.

I see gift-giving (or at least I once did) as a means to fill a gap and help people function better in life. Hey, give people something that they *need* when you have the opportunity! However, when people open a box looking for something shiny, frivolous and exciting and there they find, for example a cake plate, well, let's just say there is a let-down and disappointment that registers on the face and the voice.

Now, I'm not saying that God thinks like me or that I think like God (although I'm trying more and more to think like Him!), but when it comes to spiritual gifts (*charismata*), they are tools, not toys. They are more about function than frivolity and feel-good. They are more about God's work than our pleasure and play.

Spiritual gifts are tools that are given according to our calling. When God calls us in order to send us, He equips us through imparting spiritual gifts. These gifts are given according to His grace and according to His good pleasure.

They are true gifts. They are not earned. Although they are not cheap, they are unmerited. They are not like Christmas bonuses for which we somehow feel an entitlement. They are not like fringe-benefits that we expect. They are real "gifts"—something freely given by God to His children.

They are supernatural. Spiritual gifts are not intuition, personality traits, talents, strengths nor temperaments. They are not the result of genetics, environment or education. They are supernatural manifestations of God's Spirit in individual lives. There are those who feel that a spiritual gift is a work of grace where God takes hold of our natural abilities – talents, strengths—and ignites them for service (this view is discussed in *Gifts and Graces: A Commentary on 1 Corinthians 12-14* by Arnold Bittlinger); but I see it more in lines with John Wimber who says, "The Gifts of the Spirit are not trophies or talents, traits or toys. The gifts of the Spirit are God's supernatural expressions of love, healing and concern bestowed upon us."

Perhaps the confusion over using the term "gifts" comes when we refer to something given freely by God. We know that the "gift of salvation" is a free gift of grace, and we know that it comes with no strings attached. Since many of us don't understand the true significance of putting the words "spiritual," "grace" and "gifts" together, it creates confusion.

Russell Spittler of Fuller Theological Seminary coined the phrase "gracelets'—little bits of grace—in referring to spiritual gifts *(charismata* and *pneumatikos)*.[3] I like this word because it puts things in perspective: *gifts are little bits of grace.*

In the original Greek texts, there are several words used for "gifts" including *"domata"* and *"charismata."* In his letter to the Ephesians, Paul uses *doma* and *domata* (plural) referring to the gifts of the risen and ascended Christ as they are unfolded in diverse equipping ministries in the church. Christ Himself gives the church a diversity of services. The fundamental theme of the entire section is the unity of the church. He helps us to understand that there is a unity in variety, a unity in diversity. This necessitates the organization of the church, for it is Christ Himself who gives some to be apostles, some to be prophets, some to evangelists, pastors and teachers. They themselves— men and women—are the gifts to the church so that the church can be the gift to the world.

"Gracelets" are indeed gifts because they are freely given, yet they are tools in that they are given to assist us in assignment from God.

---

3 The word *"charismata"* is used in Romans 12:6-8 referring to the gifts and *"pneumatikos"* in *1 Corinthians 12.*

Oh yes, I have never again on special gift-giving occasions given Phyllis anything that even resembles a cake plate. Although tempted to be pragmatic, I have abbreviated my approach to gift-giving (where my wife is involved) to giving things that were sparkly or shiny or smell really good.

TOOLS NOT TOYS

In the past we have often failed to speak about spiritual gifts as important parts of the Believer's life. We made them add-on's, luxuries and accessories. There has been an emphasis on vocal gifts (speaking in tongues, interpretation, prophecy) that has made them appear to some as trivial and ego-driven. And in doing so, even though they were given by God as part of the "Grace Package" for Believers, they were often trivialized and looked upon not so much as tools but as toys.

Tools and toys are not the same. Toys are playthings used for pleasure, as a means of escape from reality and a distraction to make us feel good. Tools are used for work.

Spiritual gifts are trans-rational—overwhelming our reason—in the sense that God in His own way and purpose and at His own discretion gives them. Reason and rationale are also involved since the person involved uses them, or exercises them at his discretion (1 Corinthians 14:32, 33).

Spiritual gifts are given according to the call of God because they are tools to be used in that call. When we look at them as toys, we see them as peripheral, we see them as add-ons and unimportant, we see them as things that can be taken or left behind. When we honestly begin to see spiritual gifts as tools—necessary components to our call and ministry—we will respect them and think about them differently.

Somewhat like little Russian nesting dolls, spiritual gifts are "enclosed" in the gift of the Holy Spirit. When the Holy Spirit invades our life He brings with Him certain gifts. They are "grace gifts" that are a part of God's grace through the "gift of the Holy Spirit."

It seems to me that there are two categories of gifts: Occasional Gifts and Residual Gifts.

OCCASIONAL GIFTS

When I use the term "occasional," I refer to them as gifts given for a particular occasion. Occasional gifts are those that are listed in 1 Corinthians Chapter 12. These gifts serve as a part of God's communication with His people as they meet together. As Paul begins his inspired discourse about spiritual gifts, he does so in the context of two things: community and communication.

"Gracelets" are to be exercised in community. Christianity is not meant to accommodate a solo lifestyle; rather its very nature requires a life of accountability, with reciprocal relationships

> **Spiritual gifts are given according to the call of God because they are tools to be used in that call.**

lived out in community. In reference to occasional gifts, John Wimber says,

> *"A Believer does not possess gifts; a Believer receives gifts from God to be used at special times for special occasions. Gifts are the attestation of the empowering of the Holy Spirit and are vital in a signs and wonders ministry. Spiritual empowering equips one for service. The gifts are the tools which enable one to fulfill the ministry required. The gifts of the Spirit are received by impartation. The gifts (except the private use of tongues) are given to us and through us to use for others, and are developed in a climate of risk-taking and willingness to fail."*[4]

The church as a community of reciprocal living is important in growth and usefulness for God. And meeting together so that "gracelets" are exercised and can be judged in a loving and constructive way is a vital part of God's plan. (See Appendix 1)

But in the context of this book we will look more at the residual gifts that are given because of your call. God gifts us with residual gifts for the calling and sending He has given us. They shape us and give substance to our call in much the same way the tools of a particular profession shape and give meaning to them.

---

4   Wagner, *Church Growth: State of the Art* (Tyndale, 1986 p.149)

RESIDUAL GIFTS—TOOLS OF THE CALL

When the church planter Paul, addresses the church in Rome, he outlines other gifts that deal with function (Romans 12). Here he lists seven gifts (*charismata*):

Prophecy *(propheteia)*

Serving *(diakonia)*

Teaching *(diadasko)*

Exhorting *(parakaleo)*

Giving *(matadidomi)*

Leading *(proistemi)*

Showing mercy *(eleeo)*

These gifts are more residual than occasional. They reside within the person and are needed and useful to them because of the calling that they have received from God. These gifts are "tools of the trade" and certainly not trinkets! They give both identity and ability to carry out that which God has called and sent a person to do. God calls us and sends us but also equips us for the task that He has for us to do. Since God wants to use everybody everywhere all the time, everyone should have spiritual gifts operating in their lives. Everyone. They are not options; they are not toys.

It is interesting that prophecy/prophet is in all three listings of gifts (1 Corintnians 12:10, Ephesians 4:11, Romans 12:6). The gift of prophecy is the special God-given ability to certain members of the Body of Christ to receive and communicate an immediate message of God to His people through a divinely anointed utterance.

Prophecy is an ability to speak something that is known by the Holy Spirit, not something learned or developed. It is a gift of insight and expression. Being a prophet or having a prophetic ministry is different from having a prophecy in the church gathering. In the gathering anyone can prophesy as the Holy Spirit moves in and among those present (1 Corinthians 14:31, 32). Everyone who prophesies speaks to each other for their strengthening, encouragement and comfort (vs. 3).

There seems to be a progression: everyone can—has the ability in the gathering—to prophesy; some as cited here in Romans 12, have the gift of prophecy and some are prophets (Ephesians 4:11).

It is much the same way with serving. Everyone is required to serve others yet some have a gift—a special, over-the-top ability—to serve. Everybody is a servant, while others who are specially gifted serve as deacons *(diakoneo)*.

Everyone is called upon to teach and train someone else: the more mature teach the younger, the older women teach the young women how to love their husbands (Titus 2:4), and we all make disciples teaching them to obey and observe all Jesus' commandments (Matthew 28:18-20). But there are those who are gifted to teach and then there are those who are Teachers as part of the Ascension-gift ministries of Ephesians 4.

Each of these gifts is exercised according to the proportion of faith that we have. We both see ourselves humbly (after all this is all by grace—God doing for us what we could not do for ourselves!) and think of ourselves according to the measure *(analogia)* of faith that we have been given.

We are all supposed to give and be givers, but some actually have the *gift* of giving. (It would also seem obvious to me that those gifted to give financially would have a parallel gift of "making money" also, so that they could actually give!)

All Believers are to exhort, comfort and encourage, but some have a true gift of encouragement. And some are gifted to lead. These are particularly seen in the Ascension-gifts of Ephesians 4.

There is a definite pattern here.

GOD GIFTS US ACCORDING TO THE CALL

The calling and sending of God sets us apart for fulfillment of a particular assignment from God. This calling gives us a certain spiritual identity and certain uniqueness in the Body of Christ. It is more of a specialty in ministry than specialness to God. It is more like becoming a specialist where God has qualified you in certain areas than attempting to develop a hierarchy of authority and rank.

Spiritual gifts become God's way of dividing labor and accomplishing His plan. It is Jesus who is both the One served in the use of the gifts and the One who dispenses them.

The Ascension-gifts (often referred to as the Five-Fold ministries) is God's way of equipping and preparing the church for her redemptive mission and co-labor with God Himself. Continually being equipped and internal transformation are ongoing as we follow the Spirit in His Mission. We are transformed as we serve God and equipped as we are in community with other gifted Believers.

The Ascension-gifts—apostle, prophet, teacher, evangelist, pastor—are gifts to the church and given by the ascended Christ. These are people-gifts. They are people who have been gifted to be gifts to other people who have been gifted to be gifts! Not so much a ruling class but individuals gifted by God to serve and outfit Believers for the work each one has to do.

Martin Lloyd Jones, in referring to the *domata* of Ephesians 4:11 warns,

> *Nothing is so far removed from the Apostle's picture of the church as institutionalism and ecclesiasticism. These 'isms' are not to be found anywhere in the New Testament. Institutionalism is a denial of the picture of the church as the body of Christ, and of Christ alone as the Head, and of the Holy Spirit making and preserving this blessed unity. Ecclesiasticism is as much a denial of the scriptural teaching as is the chaos that is seen in other circles at the present hour where men set themselves up and recognise no authority whatsoever.*[5]

---

5   Martin Lloyd Jones 1984. *Christian Unity: An Exposition of Ephesians 4:1 to 16.* (Grand Rapids, MI: Baker Book House p177)

As an example of gifting and ministry, let's look at Pastoral Ministry.

A biblical understanding of a "pastor" refers to the special ability God gives to certain members of the church to assume a long-term personal responsibility for the spiritual welfare of a group of believers. These words are used in the Greek for this assignment: *"poimen"* (shepherd, pastor), *"episkopos"* (overseer, bishop), *and "presbuteros (elder)* and it would seem that the certain gifts would be evident in their lives. You could say that this mix of spiritual gifts is the very thing that makes a pastor a pastor.

- Exhortation/Encouragement (*parakaleo/paraklesis*—"to call near")—ability to minister words of comfort, consolation, encouragement and counsel in such a way that others feel helped and healed.

- Mercy (*eleeo*)—ability to feel genuine empathy and compassion for individuals (both Christian and non-Christian) who suffer distressing physical, mental or emotional problems and to translate that compassion into cheerfully done deeds that reflect Christ's love and alleviate the suffering.

- Leadership (*proistemi*—"to stand before")—ability to set goals in accordance with God's purpose for the future and to communicate these goals to others in such a way that they voluntarily and harmoniously work together to accomplish those goals for the glory of God.

- Administration/Government (*kubernesis*—"acts of helmsmanship, steering") ability to understand clearly the immediate and long-range goals of a particular unit of the body of Christ and to devise and execute effective plans for the accomplishment of those goals.

When the call of God is to pastor and shepherd other Believers, these gifts are obvious. And some pastors are more gifted prophetically; others are enriched with more *diadasko* to teach. But these gifts help make them more effective as the pastor for a specific group of Jesus-followers.

As another example, an apostle is one who is sent, not so much one who rules. (Probably those who stay and oversee groups of churches are more properly in Bible definitions "bishops" than "apostles.") The apostle is the "missionary" sent by God as the wise master builder (1 Corinthians 3:10) to lay foundations for the church to be built. The church is built on the foundations of the apostles and prophets. An apostle has an ability to "step over fences" imposed by cultures. He has an ability to utilize many gifts and release many others. It appears in the New Testament that apostles traveled with those who were gifted in other ways, especially prophets. Paul identifies himself as a teacher, herald and apostle. The apostle is the one sent and carries many different tools and gifts to accomplish His tasks.

SO, HOW DO I KNOW WHAT GIFTS I ACTUALLY HAVE BEEN GIVEN?

If indeed God gifts us according to the call and those gifts are tools that make us useful in God's plan, how do we discover those gifts? How do we know what they are so that they might be actualized and known in our lives and ministry?

Here are some ideas:

- Pray and ask God! As amazing as it seems there are many church-going, Bible-believing Jesus-followers who are unaware that God will actually communicate with them. But the truth is if you ask God, He will show or tell you what gifts are resident in you.

- Ask those who know you best. Since Christianity is never meant to be lived solo but in community, there should be people who know you and observe you, who are capable to discern and understand your gifts.

- Take a spiritual gifts survey. Some are available online.

CHAPTER 6

GOD ANOINTS ACCORDING TO THE GIFTS...

*G*od addressed Samuel: *"So, how long are you going to mope over Saul? You know I've rejected him as king over Israel. Fill your flask with anointing oil and get going. I'm sending you to Jesse of Bethlehem. I've spotted the very king I want among his sons."*

"I can't do that," said Samuel. "Saul will hear about it and kill me."

God said, "Take a heifer with you and announce, 'I've come to lead you in worship of God, with this heifer as a sacrifice.' Make sure Jesse gets invited. I'll let you know what to do next. I'll point out the one you are to anoint."

Samuel did what God told him. When he arrived at Bethlehem, the town fathers greeted him, but apprehensively. "Is there something wrong?"

"Nothing's wrong. I've come to sacrifice this heifer and lead you in the worship of God. Prepare yourselves, be consecrated, and join me in worship." He made sure Jesse and his sons were also consecrated and called to worship.

When they arrived, Samuel took one look at Eliab and thought, "Here he is! God's anointed!"

But God told Samuel, "Looks aren't everything. Don't be impressed with his looks and stature. I've already eliminated him. God judges persons differently than humans do. Men and women look at the face; God looks into the heart."

Jesse then called up Abinadab and presented him to Samuel. Samuel said, "This man isn't God's choice either."

Next Jesse presented Shammah. Samuel said, "No, this man isn't either."

Jesse presented his seven sons to Samuel. Samuel was blunt with Jesse, "God hasn't chosen any of these."

Then he asked Jesse, "Is this it? Are there no more sons?"

"Well, yes, there's the runt. But he's out tending the sheep."

Samuel ordered Jesse, "Go get him. We're not moving from this spot until he's here."

Jesse sent for him. He was brought in, the very picture of health— bright-eyed, good-looking.

God said, "Up on your feet! Anoint him! This is the one."

Samuel took his flask of oil and anointed him, with his brothers standing around watching. The Spirit of God entered David like a rush of wind, God vitally empowering him for the rest of his life.

Samuel left and went home to Ramah.

–I Samuel 16:1-13, *The Message*

⌘　⌘　⌘

God calls us.

He gifts us according to the call.

He anoints us according to the gifts.

God calls us to Himself according to His Grace, giving us specific assignments that are to be worked and lived out throughout our lifetime. As He gathers us, renews us and transforms us, He sends us.

And He gives spiritual gifts as tools to assist in carrying out our tasks. God never asks of us something He Himself does not supply. Having created everything out of nothing, He does not expect that of us! He supplies our needs for ministry through various gifts.

These gifts are often dormant and unused until God Himself calls them forward and others see them. Anointing occurs when the Holy Spirit actualizes and empowers that which He has previously deposited in us.

Anointing is both about recognition and activation. Anointing is about recognition by leadership and community. Anointing is also activation by the Holy Spirit. Both involve the setting apart for the purposes of God.

A HISTORY OF ANOINTING

Throughout the Old Testament, we see oil used as an instrument of anointing. Over and over oil is used to symbolically set apart something, some place or someone as special in service and use for God.

At Bethel, Jacob pours oil over a stone pillar following a dramatic dream and encounter with God that led to a subsequent vow to the Lord (Genesis 28:16-22). Jacob experienced God in a certain place and set it apart as significant by anointing the stone where he laid his head following a fitful night's sleep. The act of anointing set the pillar, and consequently the place as holy and set apart.

As the children of Israel journeyed in the desert from Egypt, the newly built Tabernacle, the instruments of sacrifice and the priests themselves were anointed as an act of consecration and "setting apart," dedicating them for special use. (Leviticus 8:10 and Exodus 28:41)

The anointing of the early kings of Israel was somewhat of an initiation rite for ruling. The "ministry" of a king was to lead the tribes of Israel; the anointing was the visible establishment and consecration of their leadership. In 1 Samuel 10, Samuel anointed Saul the first king and David the second. With the anointing of Saul, came the presence of the Holy Spirit.

In the Old Covenant, the Holy Spirit came and went in people's lives. He was present for certain tasks, but departed after the task was complete, or in the case of Saul when he disqualified himself for leadership.[6] This is one reason that David, following his great bouquet of sins—lust, murder, seduction, lying, etc.—cries out, *"Create in me a pure heart, O God, and renew*

---

6   1 Samuel 13:13-14; 15:10-31; 16:14

a steadfast spirit within me. Do not cast me from your presence or take your Holy Spirit from me. Restore to me the joy of your salvation and grant me a willing spirit, to sustain me" (Psalms 51:10-12). David does not want the same fate and loss of grace that he had seen in Saul.

But the life, death, resurrection and ascension of Jesus, changed that. The promised New Covenant. The prophet Jeremiah saw it coming:

"Behold, days are coming," declares the LORD, "when I will make a new covenant with the house of Israel and with the house of Judah, not like the covenant which I made with their fathers in the day I took them by the hand to bring them out of the land of Egypt, My covenant which they broke, although I was a husband to them," declares the LORD.

"But this is the covenant which I will make with the house of Israel after those days," declares the LORD, "I will put My law within them and on their heart I will write it; and I will be their God, and they shall be My people.

"They will not teach again, each man his neighbor and each man his brother, saying, 'Know the LORD,' for they will all know Me, from the least of them to the greatest of them," declares the LORD, "for I will forgive their iniquity, and their sin I will remember no more."[7]

And God spoke through Ezekiel regarding a new, internal covenant:

---

7   Jeremiah 31:31-34

...I will give you a new heart and put a new spirit in you; I will remove from you your heart of stone and give you a heart of flesh. And I will put my Spirit in you and move you to follow my decrees and be careful to keep my laws (Ezekiel 36:26-28).

Under the New Covenant, the Holy Spirit comes to the Believer, dwells in Him and carries out His purpose through him/her. Jesus promised the disciples:

"I will ask the Father, and He will give you another Counselor to be with you forever—the Spirit of truth. The world cannot accept Him, because it neither sees Him nor knows Him. But you know Him, for He lives with you and will be in you" (John 14:16, 17).

The Holy Spirit indwells the Believer permanently. He doesn't come and go depending on our feelings or our actions. He can be grieved[8] or quenched[9], but we are the Temple—the dwelling place and home—of the Holy Spirit, the new house of God. Previously, God by His Spirit resided in the Jerusalem Temple,[10] now He lives in His people. We have become the temple of God.[11] The constant indwelling presence of the Holy Spirit is at least one of the things about the New Covenant that makes it better than the Old Covenant![12] The Holy Spirit lives in us all the time wherever we are, leading us, speaking to us, encouraging us, empowering us and transforming us!

---

8   Ephesians 4:30
9   1 Thessalonians 5:19
10   Habakkuk 2:20
11   1 Corinthians 3:16; 16:19; 2 Corinthians 6:16; Ephesians 2:21-22
12   Hebrews 7:22; 8:6; 12:24

And the anointing from a New Testament standpoint is where recognition by leadership and community comes together with activation by the Holy Spirit of those gifts imparted to us by the Holy Spirit.

JESUS

Jesus is so much to us. He is the Savior, without His sacrificial death, we would have no hope for life and eternity. He is the Messiah or Christ, the anointed one for a special task. (The words "Messiah" (*mashiach*) in Hebrew and "Christ" (*christos*) in Greek mean "anointed one.")

Those things that Jesus accomplished through the crucifixion were done once and for all by Him.[13] One time for everybody; they are unrepeatable. They are eternal in their impact, significance and uniqueness. Unrepeatable.

But Jesus is also our example. Living His life as a human, He relied on the Holy Spirit in a remarkable way. Peter in speaking with Cornelius and his household explained that God had anointed Jesus with the Holy Spirit and power and that He went about doing good and healing all who were under the influence of the devil.

So, when did this anointing occur? Wasn't Jesus always the Son of God, always the Messiah?

Of course He was. But the baptism of Jesus by the baptizer John was a special occasion. At this event, the Holy

---

13   Romans 6:10; Hebrews 7:27; 9:12, 26; 10:10; 1 Peter 3:18

Spirit descended on Jesus in the obvious and observable form of a dove and a voice from heaven declared that He was indeed the Son of God.[14] This was in the sight and hearing of those around Him. No secret Messiah-ship, no secret calling and ministry. Although Jesus had been conceived by the Holy Spirit, although He had grown in His family in favor with God, the anointing of the Spirit launched Him into public ministry.

Right there, in the Jordan River, before everyone, Jesus is baptized. The Holy Spirit bodily descends; a voice declares Him as worthy to carry out the task before Him. Jesus' path is laid out pretty clearly, and being filled with the Holy Spirit, He is led into the wilderness to be tempted by the enemy (Luke 4). He moves from being the "coming Messiah" into the arena of ministry, conflict, redemption and transformation of actually being the Messiah.

Anointing is both public and internal. It happens internally as the deposit of God in us is actualized and activated, but it is a public recognition by men and women of God's call and gifting in a person's life.

Returning to Galilee in the power of the Spirit, Jesus forecasts the scope and impact of His ministry to the synagogue group in Nazareth, His hometown, by reading from the writing of Isaiah:

"The Spirit of the Lord is on me, because He has anointed Me to preach good news to the poor. He has sent Me to proclaim freedom for the

14   Matthew 3:16-17; Mark 1:10-11; Luke 3:22; John 1:32-33; 2 Peter 1:17

prisoners and recovery of sight for the blind, to release the oppressed, to proclaim the year of the Lord's favor." (Luke 4:18-19)

Jesus is the *Christos,* the Anointed One: one set aside for a task. The disciples were first called Christians *(christianos)* little anointed ones—in Antioch. Although the term possibly began as a derision ("Hey, who do those guys think they are anyway? Little Christs—*christianos?*") they functioned as those set apart for a purpose.

God anoints us according to the gifts. And the act of anointing is the place where what God has given us to do—the call—and He has gifted us to accomplish is made known both by God and the community in which we are called to minister.

HAPPENING IN COMMUNITY — ANTIOCH

In many groups and especially in the past, the recognition of what God has called and gifted a person to do was recognized by leaders and the community through a special time of ordination. Ordination is the setting apart, acknowledgement and approval of a person for the task and call God has given them.

This best happens among a community of like minded, spirit-filled Believers. We see this in the setting apart and sending out of Saul/Paul and Barnabas from the non-Jewish outsider church of Antioch (Acts 13:1-3).

The diverse group of leaders in the church in Antioch was characterized as being prophets and teachers. Ethnically they were Greeks and Jews, North Africans and it appears that Simeon was a black African. They were old and young worshiping and fasting when the Holy Spirit instructs them (probably through a prophetic word) to, *"Set apart for Me Barnabas and Saul for the work to which I have called them."* Although in the cryptic and succinct way of narrative Scripture, this declaration could be assumed

> **Anointing is both about recognition and activation. Anointing is about recognition by leadership and community. Anointing is also activation by the Holy Spirit. Both involve the setting apart for the purposes of God.**

to be a sudden revelation and somewhat of a surprise; it wasn't.

This was not a surprise to either Barnabas or Saul. Both had been involved in the church and the movement of the Spirit for a number of years. Saul had encountered the risen Christ on the highway to Damascus where he was destined to carry the Lord's name before the Gentiles and their kings and before the people of Israel (Acts 9:15). Saul—who later was renamed Paul—knew what God had called him to do, but in spite of the calling and gifting, his true impact and destiny lay dormant.

Both Saul as a young man and Barnabas, his older mentor were waiting for that time of release into ministry. Anointing is that acknowledgement by the community as well as activation by the Spirit.

So after they continued fasting and praying, they placed their hands on them and sent Saul and Barnabas off. The laying on of hands was an act of approval and a setting apart for ministry as well as an impartation of additional gifts by those church leaders.

So Saul and Barnabas, sent on their way by the Holy Spirit, went down to Seleucia and sailed from there to Cyprus. And the church and the world have never been the same.

ANOINTING IN COMMUNITY

Christianity was never intended to be a solo experience. Serving Christ must be lived out in a community of commitment and encouragement.

Regardless of its form, this group of people has a responsibility to hold those within the community accountable for their gifts and calling. The church has the wonderful and awesome task of taking Good News to those who have none. It's too big a job to be left to a few. It's about God using everybody all the time everywhere to advance His Kingdom and do good. It's about activating men and women into the God-given ministry to which they were called and sent.

The greater, both in number and magnitude, a person's spiritual gifts and giftedness and the larger their call, the greater is the anointing. The more God invests, the more responsibility there is for one to accountably be set apart for God's purposes. Walking out in everyday life an individual's call of God is an awesome and exciting responsibility.

Anointing is about recognition and activation. Anointing is about recognition by leadership and community. Anointing is activation by the Holy Spirit. Both involve the setting apart for the purposes of God. Paul writes to the Jesus-followers in Corinth:

"For no matter how many promises God has made, they are "Yes" in Christ. And so through Him the "Amen" is spoken by us to the glory of God. Now it is God who makes both us and you stand firm in Christ. He anointed us, set His seal of ownership on us, and put His Spirit in our hearts as a deposit, guaranteeing what is to come." (2 Corinthians 1:20-22)

CHAPTER 7

GOD DISCIPLINES ACCORDING TO THE ANOINTING

I have a problem when it comes to running. Or pretty much exercise in general.

I don't like to. I don't like to run. And I have friends who run. Skinny friends that say things to me like, "Runners don't fear cholesterol tests" or "Runners eat what they want all the time." And they say this with a big I-know-more-than-you-know smile.

But my problem with running is from the eighth grade. As an overweight kid in a PE class of overachievers, I was always the last guy to finish. Especially running the obligatory laps. And the coach had this sort of misguided motivation thing that said "last guy in does one more." This means that whoever finished last in pushups, chin-ups or laps does one more while everyone else rests or takes showers. So somehow I spent a lot of time doing laps. Extra laps: running around football fields, gymnasiums, tracks, campuses. Chubby me alone doing laps.

In my mind—for some odd reason—running began to equal punishment. You want to punish me, make me run.

So—even though I know I should—I just can't get enough motivation to run or jog. In my mind, running still equals punishment. And when I see a skinny runner either out in the blazing sun or numbing cold or a soaking downpour, I just shake my head, sigh and say, "You gotta love it. You just gotta love it"

And I don't.

⌘   ⌘   ⌘

PUNISHMENT OR DISCIPLINE?

Often in our minds we cannot separate "discipline" from "punishment." Even when it comes to God.

Or maybe *especially* when it comes to God.

To punish is to subject to pain, loss, confinement, death, etc., as a penalty for some offense, transgression, or fault as in *"to punish a criminal."*

I guess my eighth grade coach felt that if you came in last you must be a slacker or someone who had "criminal intent" and therefore was worthy of punishment. (*What was he thinking?*) My understanding is that somebody has to finish last, just like somebody has to finish first.

But the idea of punishing a crime prevails in our world. "You do the crime, you serve the time," is about punishment. You mess up, you pay up.

And naturally, since we in our church world have a distant relationship with God and assume He's the Big Man Upstairs—like us only bigger—He must be into punishment.

God is not into punishing His children. Punishment is a penalty for wrongdoing. Punishment is a payment for something done wrongly or with wrong intent; a criminal act. And to add to our confusion, discipline often *feels* like punishment. But God is not into punishing His children.

When we comprehend that Jesus suffered and died, not just to take us to heaven one day (as wonderful as that might be!) but so that God Himself would now deal with us as His Children, the same way He deals with Jesus, His Son. God now relates to us as His Children, as redeemed and forgiven men and women. We are no

> **Know then in your heart that as a man disciplines his son, so the LORD your God disciplines you. (Deuteronomy 8:5)**

longer outsiders, but part of His Family. The death and resurrection of Jesus was to transform who we were—the good, the bad and the ugly—into who He wants us to be and to make us useful for His redemptive purposes.

Sometimes when we forget about His amazing and astounding grace, we still see God as working to punish us for our mistakes, shortcomings and sin. We erroneously believe He makes us run laps, gives us a beating or makes us suffer ostracism as payment of our sin. As we begin to understand grace, we begin to understand God's approach through the New Covenant to us.

Grace is a different approach!

If God indeed has a destiny—a non-transferrable assignment—for every man, woman and child and if He loves us unconditionally having bestowed His grace and invested gifts in us, then discipline is about training us to excel, not about terrorizing us because we failed; God's discipline is about educating us to do better. It's about development not penalties.

The writer to Hebrew Believers reminds them:

> *And you have forgotten that word of encouragement that addresses you as sons: "My son, do not make light of the Lord's discipline, and do not lose heart when He rebukes you, because the Lord disciplines those He loves, and He punishes everyone He accepts as a son." Endure hardship as discipline; God is treating you as sons. For what son is not disciplined by his father? If you are not disciplined (and everyone undergoes discipline), then you are illegitimate children and not true sons. Moreover, we have all had human fathers who disciplined us and we respected them for it. How much more should we submit to the Father of our spirits and live! Our fathers disciplined us for a little while as they thought best; but God*

disciplines us for our good, that we may share in His holiness. No discipline seems pleasant at the time, but painful. Later on, however, it produces a harvest of righteousness and peace for those who have been trained by it. Therefore, strengthen your feeble arms and weak knees. (Hebrews 12:5-12, NIV)

Here he uses the Greek word *"paideia"* to discuss the Lord's interaction with His children. This word has as a root meaning of the whole training and education of children. *Padeia* relates to the development of intellect and ethics, mind and morals. It speaks of employing for this purpose commands and admonitions, reproof and reprimand. It means that God uses His means of disciplining us to help us grow as His children.

God's plan is to use us in His great mission. And discipline is still necessary: God calls us; He gifts us according to the call; He anoints us according to the gifts and He disciplines us according to the anointing. The greater the anointing, the greater the discipline.

The Objectives of God's Discipline

The Bible clearly states that God disciplines us because of His love and He disciplines us because we are His children. The outcome of discipline is that we might glorify Him by reflecting who He is in at least three areas:

- spiritual character
- spiritual habits
- spiritual gifts

For many years we lived in East Africa. There, one of the most common tool is a long knife-like instrument called a *panga*. The *panga* is used for everything: cutting down trees, cutting grass, opening coconuts. Everything. And because it is useful in so many areas and because young men begin using it an early age, they are very skillful. I have seen men squat with their knees around their ears and cut grass as close as a lawnmower using a *panga*. With a *panga* I have seen men take down small trees with two strategically placed whacks.

And I have seen it used in preparing a goat or a chicken for cooking. Not so much slicing the meat as chopping and whacking the pieces in preparation for the fire or the cooking pot.

But no one seems to want a new *panga*. Why? Because the new *panga*, although shiny and bright, is very dull with no edge. Not being sharp means limited usefulness. The usefulness of the *panga* comes with the sharpening. The sharper it is, the easier it is to use, and therefore more useful.

So many times I would see a man sitting by his door with a stone (or if he was well off, a file) in hand honing the edge of the *panga* preparing it for the task at hand, whether it be goats or trees. You could listen and hear the rough *scrape, scrape, scrape* of the sharpening tool rubbing against the *panga's* metal blade.

Sharpening the *panga* wears away the blunt edge reshaping and transforming it into a sharp edge ready to be used.

Discipline is not punishment but preparation. *Scrape, scrape, scrape!*

GOD DISCIPLINES US TO DEVELOP CHARACTER

Character is hard to define. But we know it when we encounter it! We know it when we find it exhibited by someone. And we realize the absence of character by the gaping hole in someone's life. Character is what you do and who you are when no one's watching. Character is what you do in the dark. Over the last few decades, we've seen public figures—political, corporate and even religious—display a tremendous lack of character. They have displayed lust, greed, ego, and evil in shocking ways. They have wronged others for their own pleasures, fortunes and advancement. Even though they espoused character, convictions and moral fiber, they displayed great weakness and were lacking in true character.

For the Believer, character is the reflection of Christ in our life. Character is godliness displayed, evident and observable in our world. Character is exhibited in daily life in the way we live, conduct our affairs and treat others. Character is exhibited in mature responses to life's situations. Character is internal but demonstrated in depth of conviction.

Discipline develops character. Character is not a gift, but is developed over years and circumstances and situations. Character is developed not implanted.

God Disciplines Us to Develop Godly Habits

Habits are those routines established in our lives. When some-thing truly becomes a habit, it is done through reflex rather than thought. I have heard that simple repetitive tasks only require a time-frame of approximately 21 days to become habit.

And when it comes to doing godly things it re-quires repetition to devel-op them into habits. For example, Bible reading and prayer. I'm convinced that

"God allows life to be rocky. His challenge is not to let the rocks grind you into dust, but to polish you to become a brilliant gem!" (from Liza, our Filipino friend in Cyprus)

one needs to have a routine of reading the Scriptures. And it requires us to become habitual about it with a goal of it be-coming "second nature" and requiring no thought process and decision-making to actually do it.

As a young man, I was wired to be a night person. I had the idea that I could study at night, read at night, enjoy life at night and do my Bible reading at night. But I encountered some people whom I considered much more spiritually mature than me, and they challenged me that if I began rising early "in the womb of the morning" (Psalm 110:3), I could not only have the "dew of my youth" but would be prepared for life's battles and find a greater fulfillment and joy in my days. So, I began arising to meet together for a time of prayer, morning devotions and Bible study at 5 a.m. The clock would go off, I'd jump up, wash my face, jump into my clothes and drive across town to meet together. This went on for five days a week for years. At first, it was a real struggle. Getting up early was not really "me," but the excitement of "meeting with God" before I began any other activities was enough motivation to get me up.

It was a discipline that has developed into a habit. I still awaken almost every morning around 5 a.m. without an alarm clock or even thinking about it at bedtime. It's a habit formed through discipline.

Habits lead to self-discipline. And God uses discipline to help us develop godly, fruitful habits.

GOD DISCIPLINES US TO DEVELOP SPIRITUAL GIFTS

Spiritual Gifts, although they are given by grace according to God's purposes, are given in a sort of "new *panga*" state in need of refinement and sharpening. They require the *scrape, scrape, scrape* of discipline to make them effective.

When we begin exercising Spiritual Gifts, we do so as a novice. We do so in faith but become more comfortable and accurate in our use as we actually use them. They become more honed and precise as we use them. Like a finely whetted *panga*, a disciplined *charisma* is useful for God's purposes.

God disciplines us to develop godly character, godly habits and spiritual gifts. How does God discipline us? How does He use discipline to transform us? There are several ways that He disciplines us.

HOW DOES GOD DISCIPLINE US?
GOD DISCIPLINES US USING HIS WORD

Paul writes to his disciple and co-worker Timothy:

But as for you, continue in what you have learned and have become convinced of, because you know those from whom you learned it, and how from infancy you have known the holy Scriptures, which are able to make you wise for salvation through faith in Christ Jesus.

All Scripture is God-breathed and is useful for teaching, rebuking, correcting and training in righteousness, so that the man of God may be thoroughly equipped for every good work. (2 Timothy 3:14-17)

God uses His Word to teach, rebuke, correct and train. When we read the Word of God, when we study the Scriptures they become a mirror to us. Not only do we see the Scriptures. We see ourselves reflected in the Scriptures. We see our shortcomings. We see our frailty we see our inability to please God, to be perfect, to do things right. The Word disciplines us by testing us.

An orthodontist is someone that straightens teeth. He uses his skill with braces and his understanding of teeth to straighten and bring into alignment crooked teeth. "Ortho" in Greek means "straight." The Greek word Paul uses to write

Timothy that we translate "correcting" is the word *"epanorthosis"* which comes from the same root word "to straighten" that we use to give a name to a specialized dentist who straightens teeth. The Scriptures, because they are God-breathed, can straighten our "crookedness" and bring us back into alignment to God's purpose.

One translation of 2 Timothy 3:14-17 says, *"All Scripture is inspired by God and is useful to teach us what is true and to make us realize what is wrong in our lives. It straightens us out and teaches us to do what is right."* (New Living Translation)

Here again we see the use of the word *paideia* to describe God's interaction in our life to train and change us.

Like looking into a mirror, God uses the Scriptures to train us. James writes in a letter to the early churches:

> *"Do not merely listen to the Word, and so deceive yourselves. Do what it says. Anyone who listens to the Word but does not do what it says is like a man who looks at his face in a mirror and, after looking at himself, goes away and immediately forgets what he looks like. But the man who looks intently into the perfect law that gives freedom, and continues to do this, not forgetting what he has heard, but doing it—he will be blessed in what he does."* (James 1:22-25)

GOD DISCIPLINES US USING HIS SPIRIT

The Holy Spirit disciplines us through His conviction. He convicts us of His righteousness, and of our unrighteousness.

He convicts us of the ideal, the perfect world of the possibilities and shows us how we fall short. The Holy Spirit disciplines us by showing us creativity and possibilities. He disciplines us by narrowing our possibilities and taking away those desires that are outside of what He wants for us.

The conviction of the Holy Spirit is often the gentle internal nudge that helps us know God's pleasure, God's plan and God's way. He disciplines us gently, yet sternly.

Conviction is not condemnation. Conviction is the deep inner sense of having done wrong. It might not "feel good' but it comes with hope. The Holy Spirit brings things to light and exposes them to us for the purpose of repentance and change. He shows us both our failures and our accomplishments. He is both the encourager and the one who convicts.

Condemnation on the other hand is the feeling that things are hopeless and change is impossible. The enemy of our soul uses condemnation to challenge our identity and cause us to feel hopeless. Condemnation debilitates us and stops forward movement and accomplishment. Condemnation is not God's method of disciplining His children.

Because we are a part of Christ's redemption, we are not part of any condemnation—past, present or future.

The Holy Spirit uses conviction not condemnation to discipline us according to the anointing and the gifts He has placed within us.

GOD DISCIPLINES US USING CIRCUMSTANCES

Paul the church-planter writes to the Believers at Rome:

> *...Since we have been justified through faith, we have peace with God through our Lord Jesus Christ, through whom we have gained access by faith into this grace in which we now stand. And we rejoice in the hope of the glory of God. Not only so, but we also rejoice in our sufferings, because we know that suffering produces perseverance; perseverance, character; and character, hope. And hope does not disappoint us, because God has poured out His love into our hearts by the Holy Spirit, whom He has given us.* (Romans 5 1-5)

Paul is reminding them that since Jesus came, we are now at peace with God. He's no longer angry and in the punishment mode. In fact, we now have access to God's grace—both of rescue and equipping—and we get excited in the hope of reflecting and glorifying God. But Paul goes on to say that we rejoice also in sufferings, trials, pressures and distress *(thlipsis)* because those problems result in perseverance and character. And that produces a non-disappointing hope.

Character and godly habits are produced through difficulties.

The mystery of Christ dwelling in us is like that. By the Holy Spirit, Jesus is here in us, but remains only seen in our character and external dealings. Character and spiritual gifts are always in need of sharpening. *Scrape, scrape, scrape.*

There are many words we use to describe circumstances: suffering, trials, tribulation, chastening, pain, difficulties, tests, afflictions, and hardships. But they all are negative circumstances over which we have limited control. Often we have no control! And we feel like unwilling victims.

> **Grace is what God does for us that we cannot do for ourselves. Grace is God's transfer of favor on us for specific purposes that God Himself knows.**

Yet God disciplines us because of His love and relationship. If we claim a relationship with God then we cannot despise or run from His discipline. Often the purpose of God is not to rescue us from our difficulties and trials, but to be with us in them using these difficulties as tools of transformation. God's discipline uses the problems to change us and produce godly character. Discipline is God's dealing with us to transform and remake us in the image of Jesus so that we might be useful for His purposes.

God in His mercy and grace uses circumstances to discipline us. Things that happen in our lives cause us to rethink who we are, who God is, what the church is all about, and how we can serve as transforming agents in our world. When things go terribly wrong—and they do—it is often God's way disciplining us.

God calls us; He gifts us according to the call. He anoints us according to the gifts and He disciplines us according to the anointing. The greater the anointing is—the greater the "setting apart"—the greater is the discipline.

Circumstances occur, and God uses them to discipline us.

Sometimes God gives us what we ask for and that in itself disciplines and corrects us. In Psalm 106, the writer gives a commentary on the desert wanderings of the children of Israel by saying that God gave them what they asked for, but sent leanness into their soul. I recently heard a story told about a dentist working with an undisciplined, obnoxious and defiant 10-year-old boy named Robert.

Robert arrived in the dental office, prepared for battle.

"Please get in the chair, young man," said the doctor.

"No chance!" replied the boy, looking the dentist in the eye.

"Son, I told you to climb onto the chair, and that's what I intend for you to do," said the dentist.

Robert stared at his opponent for a moment and then replied, "If you make me get in that chair, I will take off my clothes."

The dentist calmly said, "So, take them off."

The boy removed his shirt, undershirt, shoes and socks, and then looked up in defiance.

"All right, son," said the dentist. "Now get in the chair."

"You didn't hear me," sputtered Robert. "I said if you make me get on that chair, I will take off all my clothes."

"Okay, take 'em off," replied the man crossing his arms across his chest.

Robert proceeded to remove his pants and shorts, finally standing totally naked before the dentist and his assistant.

"Now, son, get in the chair," said the doctor.

Robert did as he was told, and sat cooperatively through the entire procedure.

When the cavities were drilled and filled, he was instructed to step down from the chair. "Give me my clothes now," said the boy.

"I'm sorry," replied the dentist. "Tell your mother that we're going to keep your clothes tonight. She can pick them up tomorrow."[15]

Sometimes, God disciplines us by giving us what we want to our total embarrassment. It causes us to move away from what we want toward what God wants.

Scrape, scrape, scrape.

GOD DISCIPLINES US USING HIS PEOPLE

God also uses men and women to discipline us. He uses His church to interact with us using their gifts, their calling and their abilities to discipline us and sharpen us for His purposes. Perhaps the best example of this is through discipleship and spiritual formation.

---

15   From *Bad Beginnings to Happy Endings*, by Ed Young, (Nashville: Thomas Nelson Publ., 1994), pp. 57-58

There are many things written about discipleship.[16] My concern is that they are often programmatic in their approach rather than relational. In North America we are often motivated by both a classroom mentality and numerical impact so we move toward something that offers that biggest "bang for the buck," hence the many programs and courses on discipleship. But true discipleship is relational and organic. Discipleship is a relationship where a more mature Believer impacts and imparts both information and life into a spiritually younger Believer leading to transformation and spiritual development.

True discipleship is about people development. It is about those who are further along in their spiritual journey working together with the Holy Spirit to explore and develop those things deposited in a "spiritually younger" individual's life and call from God. True discipleship is about learning from someone who knows more than you do and is somehow further in their walk with Christ that you.

True discipleship is intentional, not casual. Although spiritual formation is happening whether in a Christian biblical way or another, our spiritual values, understanding and perspective are being shaped and formed. But true Jesus-kind of discipleship must be intentional. It must involve people

---

16   Here are a few books currently available regarding disciple-making – Robert, Coleman, *The Master Plan of Evangelism* (Old Tappan, NJ: Revell, 1963); Rick Warren, *The Purpose-Driven Life* (Grand Rapids, MI: Zondervan, 2002); A.B. Bruce *The Training of the Twelve: Exhibiting the Twelve Disciples of Jesus under Discipline for the Apostleship* (New Canaan, CT: Keats Publishing, 1979; first published 1841); Bill Hull, *The Complete Book of Discipleship* (Denver, CO: NavPress, 2006)

who both know they are discipling someone and that some-one actually knows they are being discipled. There has been a mutual understanding of access to each other's life.

True discipleship is measurable and apparent. In Matthew 28:18-20 Jesus was speaking to those accompanying Him to the place of His ascension. "All authority in heaven and on earth has been given to me," He said. "Therefore go and make disciples of all ethnic groups, baptizing them and teaching them to obey everything I have commanded you." He gave instructions about both where to go and what to teach. It was not a nebulous assignment. Either they went or they stayed. Either they taught or they didn't. Whether one is being discipled or is making disciples is obvious. Either one is or one is not.

The discipleship journey to maturity involves measurable progress. Recent converts should not be considered for leadership but those recent converts should not remain as babies tossed about by everything that comes down the pike. They are to grow up and become useful in their world.

The goal of being a disciple is to develop intimacy with God—to better understand and experience who He is; to develop a better understanding of personal spiritual identity and an improved understanding of personal ministry. This happens in relational spiritual formation.

Disciples are made, not born. We have confused converts with disciples and have made "conversion" easy and abstract. As we reclaim the concept of personal discipleship, accountability and *scrape, scrape, scrape* of transformation, the church will change. And the world will be changed.

Spiritual formation occurs when disciples follow others as they themselves follow Christ.[17] Paul makes it clear that those who he discipled should closely follow His example and way of life, as he followed the example of Christ. As a disciple-maker, he opened his life and was transparent in spiritual things and in everyday life.

Personal discipleship gives the disciple-maker permission to "come alongside" to address issues of immaturity in the disciple's life. The objective of discipleship is found in Galatians 4:19—that Christ be formed in us, that we reflect Jesus in attitude, motive and action. The reason we allow others to speak and have accountability in our lives is the need for deep transformation.

In a world where self-help has become part of our self-preservation and protection mindset, allowing others access to one's life and a corresponding voice in that life is somehow foreign and strange. But it is at the core of Jesus' purpose and plan.

God calls us. He gifts us according to the Call. He anoints us according to the Gifts. And He disciplines us according to the anointing.

Scrape, scrape, scrape.

---

17   I Corinthians, 4:16, 11:1; Philippians 3:17; 1Thessalonians 1:6; 2 Thessalonians 3:9

CHAPTER 8

GOD USES US ACCORDING TO HIS PLAN AND PLEASURE...

Some years ago when Phyllis and I were living in Nairobi, Kenya, I served as director of a Bible school out in the hills near Ongata Rongai. I worked with a great staff of dedicated and very qualified Africans.

One Saturday morning the phone at our home rang very early. Answering the phone, an unfamiliar voice greeted me and began to make inquiries about who I was and my ministry in East Africa. After a few moments of conversation, the caller asked me a question, *"Will you come and teach our leaders? Our group was begun many years ago out in Western Kenya. Our forefathers wanted nothing to do with white missionaries so they took those things that we believed as Africans and married them together with parts of the Bible. But now that many of our young men can read, they are reading the Bible for themselves. And they are confused. Some of the things they have been taught do not seem to be the things that they read in the Bible. Will you come and teach our leaders the truth?"*

Well, I was a little overwhelmed. Overwhelmed, because I was aware of the group that he was talking about. They were pretty much a cult, synchronistic in their interpretation of Christianity, and really odd in their practice. So I said to my caller, *"Let me get back to you. Let me pray about this and speak with my colleagues, and you can call me next week."*

So bright and early on Monday morning I drove to the Bible school to talk with the staff there. As we sat in the office between classes drinking chai (tea), I brought up the subject of my phone call. And as I mentioned the group, it got very, very quiet in the room. In Africa pretty much all you have is your reputation, what people think of you and how they feel about you as a person. I was very much concerned that working with such an outspoken and visible cult could really destroy both my reputation and ministry. So clearing my throat, I asked them, *"What should I do?"*

It got hear-a-pin-drop quiet and as I looked around the room no one made eye contact with me. They were all looking at the floor.

Except Isaiah Dau, the principal of the school. Isaiah was a Sudanese refugee. By tribe/people group, he was a Dinka and had become a Believer after fleeing the civil war in Sudan. Like most Dinkas, he was extremely tall, extremely thin and extremely black. He was so black, that the other Africans referred to him as "the Black Man." That's black. He was so tall and skinny that when he crossed his legs it seemed to take him minutes rather than seconds to do so. And Isaiah also was very austere. He almost always wore a dark suit and tie and although he had a big smile, you didn't often see it. His facial expression was usually austere and serious. And besides that, he was blind in one eye so you were never really sure if he was looking at you.

But while everyone else was looking at the floor, I was pretty sure Isaiah was looking at me. And the question, *"What should I do?"* seemed to hang in the air.

Breaking the silence, Isaiah said to me very matter of fact, *"If you don't go, who will go? They didn't ask me, they asked you. So if you don't go, who will go? If you don't go, how will their doctrine ever change? If you don't go, how will they ever know the truth?"*

That pretty much answered my question. We began a quarterly Bible school out in Western Kenya specifically for this group, and we saw changes in their doctrine and their practice.

Isaiah Dau's question—*"If you don't go, who will go?*—still rings in my ears.

⌘   ⌘   ⌘

God calls us...
He gifts us according to the Call...
He anoints us according to the Gifts...
He disciplines us according to the Anointing...
He uses us according to His Plan and Pleasure...

Being useful to God and God's purpose in the earth is not just happenstance. Usefulness does not just indiscriminately fall out of the sky. It is neither random nor earned. Usefulness is not the result of our praying and fasting and self-denial. (Not that prayer, fasting and self-denial are not tools of discipline to hone our usefulness. Don't misunderstand me.) No, our usefulness and our being used by God is according to His purpose and His plan, His choice and His investment.

God invests Himself in His People that together in a mystical, yet practical union, His great mission can be accomplished in the earth.

As we've seen before, Paul writes to the Believers in Ephesus:

"For it is by grace you have been saved, through faith—and this not from yourselves, it is the gift of God –not by works, so that no one can boast. For we are God's workmanship, created in Christ Jesus to do good works, which God prepared in advance for us to do." (Ephesians 2:8-10)

Paul's emphasis is on the fact that it is God's grace—not our actions—that brings us salvation and puts us back into right connection with God. This relationship cannot be earned. It cannot be bought with good works, no matter how good or meritorious or sacrificial. Salvation is the result of God's grace being extended to us—and our response to receive it by faith. And even that faith is not self-generated, but is a gift from God.

The result of God's grace is that we are God's workmanship—His poetry—created to carry out activities that were prepared in advance by God for us to do.

As fellow-workers with God, we are carrying out His plan and desires. He uses us according to what He wants, not so much what we want. Our usefulness is not in our own eyes, but in His perspective. When we fit our plans into His plan, when we join our story into His story, we find usefulness and fulfillment.

God calls us and gives us unambiguous tasks. These involve specific persons, places and times, taking a lifetime to live out. It is a journey of miles and minutes, people and personalities. It is a journey of heart, attitude and love. It involves God's supernatural intervention and intrusion into our lives through spiritual gifts, anointing, "setting a-parts," and disciplines. He also uses people. People, who walk beside us, encourage us, dream with us, believe with us, criticize us and even sometimes abandon us, make us who we are. There is a supernatural interaction between us, the community of Believers and God Himself.

Living the Plan of God is "walking out" what has been placed in our hearts and lives.

Living out The Call of God is living out "The Work" of God.

GOD'S WORK—GOD USES US
AS HE DESIRES

Jesus is the master storyteller. Over and over he tells Middle
Eastern stories to teach universal truths and help His listeners
understand deep things on His heart. In the Gospel of Matthew,
Jesus tells twelve parables about the Kingdom of God. Some
speak of the nature of the Kingdom[18] and some speak of the
value of the Kingdom[19] but many speak about Kingdom stewardship[20] and our part in the work of God.

In the stewardship parables, Jesus continually speaks of a land-
owner, ruler or king who leaves his wealth and property in the
hands of those he considers worthy, leaves and unexpectedly re-
turns. We could read these stories as "attention-getters" both for
the Jews to whom He spoke and for us as His church. For the Jews,
it's about their failure in faithfulness to oversee God's Covenant.

And for us—as Jesus' church—we can see these parables
this way: Jesus has come, He has established His Kingdom[21]
and He has left us as stewards, in charge of that Kingdom until
His return.

In Matthew 25, Jesus tells the parable that we have come to
refer to as "the one about the talents." In it Jesus tells the classic

---

18 Mustard Seed (Matthew 13:31-32; Leaven (Matthew 13:33-35); Dragnet (Matthew 13:47-51)
19 Hidden Treasure, Pearl (Matthew:13:44-46)
20 Unmerciful Servant (Matthew 18:21-35); Vineyard and Laborers (Matthew 20:1-16), Marriage Feast (Matthew 22:1-14); Wise and Foolish Virgins (Matthew 25:1-13); Talents (Matthew 25:14-30)
21 Matthew 4:17; 23

story of leaving someone with responsibility and returning expecting a report.

He puts it this way:

> *Again, it—the Kingdom of God—will be like a man going on a journey, who called his servants and entrusted his property to them. To one he gave five talents of money, to another two talents, and to another one talent, each according to his ability. Then he went on his journey.*
>
> *The man who had received the five talents went at once and put his money to work and gained five more. So also, the one with the two talents gained two more. But the man who had received the one talent went off, dug a hole in the ground and hid his master's money.*
>
> *After a long time the master of those servants returned and settled accounts with them. The man who had received the five talents brought the other five. "Master," he said, "you entrusted me with five talents. See, I have gained five more."*
>
> *His master replied, "Well done, good and faithful servant! You have been faithful with a few things; I will put you in charge of many things. Come and share your master's happiness!"*
>
> *The man with the two talents also came. "Master," he said, "you entrusted me with two talents; see, I have gained two more."*
>
> *His master replied, "Well done, good and faithful servant! You have been faithful with a few things; I will put you*

in charge of many things. Come and share your master's happiness!"

Then the man who had received the one talent came. "Master," he said, "I knew that you are a hard man, harvesting where you have not sown and gathering where you have not scattered seed. So I was afraid and went out and hid your talent in the ground. See, here is what belongs to you."

His master replied, "You wicked, lazy servant! So you knew that I harvest where I have not sown and gather where I have not scattered seed? Well then, you should have put my money on deposit with the bankers, so that when I returned I would have received it back with interest.

"Take the talent from him and give it to the one who has the ten talents. For everyone who has will be given more, and he will have an abundance. Whoever does not have, even what he has will be taken from him. And throw that worthless servant outside, into the darkness, where there will be weeping and gnashing of teeth." (Matthew 25:14-30)

There are several words that stand out in this story: ability, entrusted, faithful.

THE MASTER'S INVESTMENT

Each servant—or we might say "employee"—was entrusted with different numbers of "talents." One "talent" (probably of silver) has a monetary value of around twenty years' wages. So the employee receiving five talents has enough to support

GOD USES US ACCORDING TO HIS PLAN

himself for one hundred years, or a very large amount of cash! The worker given two talents has enough for 40 years and the staffer with the single talent has a cash value of 20 years' wages. Any way you look at it, it was a substantial investment by the "man who went on the journey."

But the absentee landlord is not haphazard in his financial disbursement. He gives responsibility over his goods according to each man's "ability." The Greek word used in the New Testament is "*dunamis*" that is most often translated "power." He entrusted his goods to them according to their power to care for his goods. It was a venture done with several things in mind.

First, the master expected a return on his investment. It's obvious that on his homecoming, he anticipated there being a profit that would be more than just his initial investment. He is expecting each worker to actually work with what was given so that there might be an increase. For the landlord, faithfulness was seen as fruitfulness. For the master, doing well was exhibited by increase. He had invested with a purpose. And that purpose was that there might be more upon his arrival than there was on his departure.

Often for the church, we have seen faithfulness as maintaining, not losing. We have seen ourselves—both as individuals and congregations—as "okay" if we've maintained and did not lose. We, like the employee with the single talent, have seen "non-loss" as victory. We've felt that being able to give back that which we were given—intact, unscathed and fresh from the ground where we have preserved it is good enough. We've somehow concluded that if we maintained and didn't "retrograde" we were doing alright. Somehow we've developed the attitude that if we just "show up" we get credit.

But the master uses harsh language to reprimand the employee who basically had lost nothing and merely maintained. After calling him a wicked, lazy and worthless servant, the master has his talent taken away and given to the successful worker, saying *"For everyone who has will be given more, and he will have an abundance. Whoever does not have, even what he has will be taken from him."*

> **God invests Himself in His People that together in a mystical, yet practical union, His great Mission can be accomplished in the earth.**

Now, I'm thinking this is not doing much for this worker's self-image and self-esteem. But the master has entrusted according to the ability of each worker. He assessed the *dunamis* of each one to gain more and has entrusted as he saw fit. But because the investment and the return are so substantial and so important, this parable is about the master, his plan and his joy. The master has invested expecting multiplication and dividends and the worthless servant is the one who does not increase.

Maintenance is not enough. Just preserving is not enough. The master expects more. Where there is a divine investment, more is expected than is deposited!

Also, the master invested expecting a resulting partnership. Faithfulness is the ability to take what has been entrusted and through faith and perseverance and sheer risk produce more. It was the master's intent that these employees share in his wealth and profit.

One of the problems of the unfaithful servant is that he had no real relationship with the master. He saw the master as a "hard man" who somehow harvested from fields where he had not sowed. He saw himself as a bad field—a poor investment— and he was fearful. And his fear kept him from fulfillment. His fear kept him from profit and from entrance into partnership with the master, sharing his joy.

GRACE INVESTMENT FOR THE KINGDOM

God calls us, gifts us according to the call, anoints us according to the gifts and disciplines us according to the anointing. Each of these acts are grace investments by God in us for His purpose. Each of these is done so that we might fulfill our part in His mission.

And He expects us to respond with faith in faithfulness, risking failure for His purposes.

I have often wondered what would have been the attitude of the master if one of the workers had made a *bad investment* and lost the talents. Because you see, *nobody actually lost anything.* Everything that was entrusted was returned. Nothing was lost; there was no loss. Every talent was accounted for and returned. The loss was in increase and profit.

My sense is that had there been a loss, the master would have understood and applauded the attempt. You spell biblical faith, r-i-s-k. The concern of the master was that the lazy servant had failed in investment, not in profit. Personally, I would rather fall down moving in the right direction of faith than to stand in doubt and safety.

When God invests in us, it is for a Kingdom return. When God invests in us, it is not just for us to rest in our forgiveness, but it is for us to become active participants with Him in His Kingdom mission of redemption.

SEEING OURSELVES AS FELLOW-WORKERS IN GOD'S WORK

Now of course, Jesus is not 100% an absentee landlord. Although He is not bodily present so that we can see Him and touch Him, He is both with us and in us (John 14:20). Jesus is everywhere as the omnipresent God, but particularly in us as the indwelling Holy Spirit and mysteriously present and with us when we gather together (Matthew 18:28). We are God's *sunergos*, translated from the Greek to mean, "fellow workers" (I Corinthians 3:9). He is both working in us and through us.

And He is always working ahead of us. We are listening and watching so that we might catch up with what the Holy Spirit is doing in the world. Often we talk about "waiting on the Lord," as if somehow we are on a street corner anxiously looking at our watch wondering where He is and why He's late. We're waiting on Him to act and to do something; maybe answer our requests. In actuality, however, it seems that God is waiting on us. He has sent His Son to forgive our sins, eliminate our guilt and remove our shame. He has sent His Spirit to energize and empower us. He has called us unto Himself and gifted us with amazing supernatural gifts. He is sending us as the Sent People of God to speak His words and to do the good works, which God prepared in advance for us to do.

Since He is working everywhere, all the time among both Believers and non-believers, our best questions are always, *"What are you doing here, Lord? Can I be a part of it?"* Our goal is to be working the works that we have been equipped to do.

Jesus is our example. He was continually concerned about pleasing the Father by His actions and work. He saw Himself as working together with God the Father, not separate from Him but an extension of the Father. God was certainly not the far away Watchmaker in the sky!

Jesus was doing what the Father had sent Him to do. Jesus said to some who criticized Him for healing on a non-prescribed workday, *"My Father is always at His work to this very day, and I, too, am working."* (John 5:7). Since God is always at work, Jesus saw His own work as a 24/7/365 lifestyle. He didn't have to go somewhere special either to see God work or to work Himself. He saw Himself as anointed and set apart to do the works of God. What He did—His actions, His work –validated the fact that He was sent by God. When compared to His martyred cousin, John the baptizer, Jesus said, *"I have testimony weightier than that of John. For the very work that the Father has given me to finish, and which I am doing, testifies that the Father has sent me.* (John 5:36)

Jesus regarded The Work as that which He was sent to do. For Jesus, to complete this work brought glory and honor to the Father. (John 17:4)

After miraculously feeding 5,000 followers, Jesus ran away to the mountains avoiding the crowd's acclamation. And after being left behind by the disciples, He caught up to them by walking on the choppy sea. But the crowds followed Him and getting hungry again began to ask Him questions about what He was doing and how they could also do these things. Jesus responded to their enquiries:

"Do not work for food that spoils, but for food that endures to eternal life, which the Son of Man will give you. On Him God the Father has placed His seal of approval." Then they asked Him, *"What must we do to do the works God requires?"* Jesus answered, *"The work of God is this: to believe in the one He has sent."* (John 6:27-28)

GOD USES US ACCORDING TO HIS PLAN

As followers of Jesus, we have been given good and important works to carry out. Those works are not on some sort of celestial checklist that God is perusing from some grand throne room in the sky. They are not some preordained uphill death march to be executed daily. But more like a wonderful dance with God where we work together with Him in His endeavors. We become His hands and feet, and extension of His love and grace. We become the Good News of God with skin.

The works of God that we do are more like the pieces of the great mission of redemption fitted together by God according to the Gifts and Callings that have been deposited in us.

The "good works" that we do becomes "The Work" that God has for us to do.

We have sometimes faltered and stumbled at good works, even at the Golden Rule—*do unto others as you would have them do unto you.* Maybe it seems hard and difficult and uncomfortable. I remember an incident not long ago in an airport somewhere. While waiting at the luggage carousel there was a young mother with two small children in tow and one sleeping in her arms. She struggled attempting to get her enormous bags off a moving platform and not lose children in a bustling crowd. I walked over to her and said, "Please, let me help you." Now in most airports women who are traveling alone (or even with small children) are squeamish about being helped by strangers. I saw the look in her eyes. So, I said to her with a smile, "Let me help you, because if my wife and children were in your situation, I'd want someone to help them." I went across the room and got a cart, got her bags and put them on and helped her out the door toward a cab. *Do unto others as you would have them do unto you.* No big deal – but somehow glorifying the Father by working the good works we were created in Christ Jesus to do.

SEEING "THE WORK" AS OUR PART OF GOD'S MISSION

Jesus saw Himself as having a work to do. And Paul knew he had an assignment for God. As we discussed earlier, Paul had encountered the risen Christ on the highway to Damascus where he was destined to carry the Lord's name be-

> **Jesus is our example. And He was continually concerned about pleasing the Father by His actions and work.**

fore the Gentiles and their kings and before the people of Israel (Acts 9:15).

This becomes "The Work" for which Paul expends his life and energy. We see this in the sending out of Paul and Barnabas from Antioch to do the work of God in Acts 13. They were worshiping and fasting when the Holy Spirit instructs them to, *"Set apart for Me Barnabas and Saul for the work to which I have called them."*

Paul saw himself set apart by the Holy Spirit for "The Work." This "Work" is recognized by the church at Antioch and with their blessings, Paul and Barnabas are sent to work the works that constitute The Work. The Work is not one big thing that Paul was to accomplish and then wipe his forehead saying, "Whew, I'm glad I'm finished with that!" No, God had called, gifted, anointed, disciplined and sent Paul to do the works day by day that constituted The Work. And he was serious about doing it and completing it.

Paul considered The Work God had given him to do as something bigger than himself and as a divine trust. Paul's Work was part of the bigger Work that God was doing in the earth.

When Antioch sent out Paul and Barnabas, Barnabas' nephew John Mark accompanied them on the first part of their trip, but left them in Pamphylia. Paul saw John Mark's departure from his and Barnabas' missionary journey not just as a personal desertion, but abandonment of The Work (Acts 15:38).

Paul urged the Roman believers not to destroy The Work by wrong and divisive attitudes. He was concerned that The Work could be destroyed over people's concerns about what to eat when and where (Romans 14:20). Seemingly small things can wreck The Work. Paul urges Believers in Corinth to *"... stand firm and let nothing move you. Always give yourselves fully to the work of the Lord, because you know that your labor in the Lord is not in vain."* (1 Corinthians 15:58)

When we work the works that constitute The Work, we see our part in something bigger than we could ever conceive ourselves.

CHAPTER 9

SO, WHERE DO WE GO

FROM HERE?

God Calls →	God Gifts according to the Call →	God Anoints according to the Gifts →	God Disciplines according to the Anointing →	God Uses for His Purposes

⌘ ⌘ ⌘

God's intention is to use everybody all the time everywhere for His purpose. He desires to fill the earth with His glory, restoring creation through redeemed people. He's on a mission and He's passionate about it and will not rest until He sees it fulfilled.

And yes, you are involved. You are wanted. You are enlisted.

The reason God thinks He can use you is not because you are so special (although you are) or because you are tall, dark and handsome or short, blonde and beautiful. The reason He thinks He can use you, and that you are useable in His plan and purpose, is because of His loving investment of grace in you.

You are valuable and useful to God because God sees you as useful and has invested in you accordingly.

As we have discussed, all this is a matter of grace. It's a matter of God doing for you what you cannot do for yourself. It's a matter of His costly investment in you as you believe Him and allow Him access to your life.

Again, God calls us... He gifts us according to the Call... He anoints us according to the Gifts... He disciplines us according to the Anointing... and He uses us according to His Plan and Pleasure.

LEARNING TO LIVE ON MISSION

So, how do we move on from here? If all this is true, does this mean there's one more giant spiritual mountain to climb in the 20 minutes of extra time you have in your busy schedule? Does it mean there will be another meeting at church that you have to attend and listen intently and take copious notes? Does this mean that you have to whisk yourself off to deepest darkest Africa immediately, live in a mud hut and eat bugs? Does this mean you have to sell your new HDTV and La-Z-Boy?

Maybe.

Or maybe not. I am sure that all this is not about some new mountain to climb or some new spiritual frustration. It's about discovery! It's about joining your story to God's story. It's about reworking you heart and mind to understand you are part of God's redemption plan. And it is about seeing from a new perspective. Where you stand will always determine what you see.

And the way you see yourself, will determine what you actually do.

CHOSEN

God chooses us and sends us. He began this sending process with the first disciples and continues it with us. He said to them, *"When the Holy Spirit comes on you, you will be able to be My witnesses in Jerusalem, all over Judea and Samaria, even to the ends of the world."* (Acts 1:8)

Election—God's choice, God's call—is not so much about who gets to go to heaven; election is about whom God chooses to be part of His crisis-response team to bring healing to the world: Jerusalem, Judea, Samaria and the uttermost parts of the earth.

"Jerusalem" is your hometown. "Jerusalem" is where you are right now. It's the place you buy your groceries, pump your gasoline and cut your grass. It's your neighborhood, your street and the people you see when you go to the mailbox.

Probably those people have some concept of Christianity. They speak the same language you do and probably have similar interests. There's a good chance they are of the same nationality, the same ethnic group and are from a class grouping similar to yours or those of your church.

Your "Judea" might be the average non-Christian: a person or people-group that has little real awareness of or interest in Christianity as they know it. They are suspicious of the church because they have heard bad things. These people might be politically correct, socially aware, and open to spirituality. Or they might have been previously offended by a bad experience of church attendance or had angry run-ins with Christians. You could go to the average local pub/bar or nightclub to encounter these people. Or even Wal-Mart.

We might categorize "Samaria" for you as the people who have absolutely no idea about Christianity and what it means to follow Jesus. They might be part of an ethnic group with different religious backgrounds or some fringy subculture. This category might include people who feel marginalized by evangelical Christianity—for example the gay community or wiccans. But "Samaria" will definitely include people actively antagonistic toward Christianity as they understand it.

And they might be in your location or they might be way across the world. The "uttermost" will include a group who might be inhabited by ethnic and religious groupings like Muslims or Jews or Hindus. Just about everything gets in the way of a meaningful dialogue with these groups. They are highly resistant to the Gospel because of their own collection of stereotypes and misunderstandings. They have built their own mental and emotional zone of truth and territory of comfort. But we are sent to take them good news. Our task as the sent people of God, is to personify acceptance, understanding and demonstrate God's love and grace.

Some years ago when we were transitioning from East Africa to North Africa, we spent a year in the USA refueling and retooling. At the school my daughter attended it became known that we were a missionary family. One day she was belligerently confronted by a misunderstanding eighth-grader, *"What right do you have to go to another country and force people to change their religion?"*

Good question if that was what we were doing. What right, indeed. We were not forcing anybody to do anything, but simply offering a better life and genuine relationship with God through Jesus Christ. And we couldn't care less about religion—empty religion is merely an attempt to know God on our own terms, whether it's in a church or in a mosque or a temple! And there's the rub. People are so used to being targets of a religious evangelism rather than the objects of our love and compassion that they bristle at the very presence of followers of Jesus! The reason people are resistant to the "Gospel" is that we've not told them and lived out among them the beauty of "Good News." Jesus is the Door, not the wall. He's not about keeping people out. He's about letting people in—into right standing with God; into a life of communion and communication with the Creator! Into a life of joy, not constant angst and frustration! The wall of separation had been there, but Jesus' coming blasts a wonder filled doorway allowing people come to God, where there is joy unspeakable and where their deep hope is actualized!

And going to them with good news is part of our call.

God has placed inside us solutions for the world around us. When we look at ourselves and understand our gifts and callings—God's investment in us—we can find solutions. The gifts given to us are tools of redemption, not toys. They are given so that we can live our lives in joy and passion. They add value to those around us.

We find our identity internally through God's deposit. Gifts, callings and anointing mold us and make us who we are. We have to stop looking for God to fall out of the sky and show up in our meetings. He promises to be there already, so we must stop talking like He's not. He promises to be among us, never leaving nor forsaking. And He promises to manifest Himself through these "gracelets."

Paul writes to the Believers in Rome:

> *For there is no difference between Jew and Gentile—the same Lord is Lord of all and richly blesses all who call on Him, for, "Everyone who calls on the name of the Lord will be saved." How, then, can they call on the One they have not believed in?*

And how can they believe in the One of whom they have not heard? And how can they hear without someone preaching to them? And how can they preach unless they are sent?

As it is written, "How beautiful are the feet of those who bring good news!" (Romans 10:12-15)

Theologian John Stott says, *"Mission is the global outreach of the global people of a global God."* [22] Around the corner or around the world, we are living on a mission, participating in God's mission.

But God's call and His mission are not nebulous and filled with unreal obligations and expectations. God gives us tools to carry out everything He gives us to do. We are empowered by His Spirit and guided by God's loving community. We are part of God's reconciliation team in the earth for the sake of the Kingdom.

We're living out our destiny: living and bringing good news!

Let me give you some "We've Got To's."

WE'VE GOT TO BEGIN THINKING LIKE MISSIONARIES

Thinking missionally, we must move our focus from inward to outward. It's not only about us. I'm not saying your needs and healing and well-being are unimportant. I'm saying that we have a tendency to be focused on ourselves. (Just let someone

---

22   John Stott, *The Contemporary Christian: An Urgent Plea of Double Listening* 1992, p.335

take a group photo. Who do we search for first as it's passed around?) Focusing outwardly is both about laying our interests aside and embracing a bigger interest – God's. It's not simply about our needs and our wants and our hurts and our pleasure—for God knows we have needs; He will supply them. And as for our pleasure—we will find total satisfaction and joy as we find our place in His plan for redeeming a broken world!

But the opposite of being "missional" is to be "stational." I know this sounds ridiculous to say, but the opposite of actually "going" is actually "staying." And in doing so, we become merely consumers, rather than missionaries. Rather than going to those in need, we can be more comfortable "ordering in" from God and enjoying all the benefits ourselves. Somehow, comfort, convenience and safety can become our priority. Our focus must change!

We can no longer—whether in North America or northern Thailand—continue to think we can attract people to come and see what we're doing. God wants to use you to go where He is already working, to answer the questions that people there are already asking and to be a "witness" of what you have seen and heard.

For so long in North America, we've lived in a world that was not really hostile to the church or the Gospel. (Oh, we always said it was, but it really wasn't.) Most of our institutions—courts, schools, colleges, and government—have been shaped by Judeo-Christian values and touched by evangelical Christianity. We could talk about "getting saved" or use biblical analogies (like David and Goliath, or "walking on water") and the culture understood what we meant. Most people knew they needed Jesus and we just exhorted them to "do what they knew they should do." Many people recognized the church as a legitimate voice in the community and showed respect. But things have shifted. The world has changed. We—as the church—have lost our "home field advantage" and rather than adapting and understanding the changes, I find that many church people and church leaders are just angry about it. Longing for the good old days, they look at legislation, boycotts and protests to change the society back to the way it was. They are angry at all the new stakeholders (such as gays, immigrants with different religions, atheists) in the new world. Rather than looking for ways to relate to the world as it is, they keep longing for the world "like it used to be."[23]

Missionaries must have a different, forward-thinking mindset. They are on a mission with God and know that the society they enter will hold different values, different family systems, different perspectives and love different things that they do.

---

23 Michael Wolff, *New York Magazine*, Feb 26 2001, p.19 *"...we are at the fundamental schism in American cultural, political, and economic life. There's the quicker-growing, economically vibrant, but also more fractious and more difficult to manage, morally relativist, urban-oriented, culturally adventuresome, sexually polymorphous, and ethnically diverse nation... And there's the small-town, nuclear-family, religiously oriented, white-centric other America, which makes up for its diminishing cultural and economic force with its predictability and stability...."*

They are there to both adapt and to speak to that world. And in the tradition of "lighting one candle" rather than "cursing the darkness," they learn how to relate to their new world.

Speaking in a church recently I mentioned the huge influx of Muslims and Hindus into our part of the world. Following the service, a young man came up to me and asked me rather skeptically where they were, how he could find them and how could he begin ministering to them. I smiled and said, "You know the intersection near the church? There is a pharmacy on one corner and two convenience stores on the other two, right? If you go in the Shell station, the guy there is a Muslim. The family that runs the other store is Hindu."

"How do you know that?" he asked, "and how can I minister to them?"

"I know by their names—Muslim names are different from Hindu names. If you want to minister to them, begin paying cash for your gas. Go in there twice a week, greet him and after a few times ask him about his family. Introduce yourself. He'll ask about your family. Tell him. Don't hand him a tract or talk about church, talk about life for a few minutes. After several months of going there and paying higher gas prices than Wal-Mart and taking the time to chat with him, ask him to come to your house for a meal. Become his friend with no ulterior motive. Learn who he is. Be his friend. Let God take care of the rest."

When we think like missionaries, we respect the people around us who are not like us. We respect the way their particular hardships have shaped their worldview and hindered their path to Truth. And we recognize their "lostness" in a sympathetic, non-patronizing way. Thinking like missionaries helps us to empathize and know what it's like not to believe. We seek to relate to those whose lives are dented, scratched, bruised, and shamed. We seek to live making a relevant connection to the God of all comfort.

My friend Mike recently told me he was trying very hard to think more like a missionary.

Through a series of events, a small struggling congregation in a rural community asked his assistance in looking for a new way to reshape their world. My friend asked them to pray about who they would like to impact in their neighborhood. After a few days they returned saying they wanted to interact with and bring good news to the growing Vietnamese population in their area, but they were unsure where to begin.

Mike took our Vietnamese-American friend Tom who thinks both like a missionary and an evangelist to visit the community. Thinking like a missionary, he said, "First we have to find an inroad to the Vietnamese community. I know three things about the Vietnamese: they usually don't cook so well, so they won't open a restaurant; they won't fight against the Chinese "mafia" so they usually won't open a grocery store; thus they usually open a nail salon. So let's ask around and see where there might be a nail shop."

Sure enough, there was a nail salon within a few hundred yards of the church building.

Stopping by, Mike and Tom discovered that the shop was run by two Vietnamese sisters. Upon entering, Tom began to converse with the ladies in Vietnamese listening to their stories of how they came to this community and the influx of other Vietnamese into the area. One continued telling of the plight in which she now found herself with a less than supportive live-in boyfriend. Within a few minutes, she was weeping and relating her struggles in Vietnamese to a listening Tom. She was weeping so loudly that a customer asked my friend what he was doing to cause such uproar. My friend gently replied, "I'm just speaking to this lady in her heart language and listening to her story. I hope we're not disturbing you." With a nod, she closed her eyes and tuned out the conversation.

Tom was thinking like a missionary. He was "turned on" to the world around him.

If we are to see the world as missionaries, we must see it as it is and become engaged with it. As a missionary we seek to understand cultural patterns and look for entrances into the lives of those around us. Listening, we earn the right to speak.

WE'VE GOT TO BE BLESSINGS TO THOSE UNLIKE US

Like Abraham of old, we have been blessed to be a blessing. He was told that all people unlike him were to be blessed through him. We all are to be blessings to people not of our family, tribe or kindred.[24] But if we hide ourselves away and expect others to minister the grace of Jesus Christ, or expect the professionals to do the ministry, we will never be a blessing. We are gifted to give and to serve others. We must intentionally begin blessing others.

We must begin serving with a no-strings-attached attitude, not driving any hidden agenda. People are suspicious of agendas. People are scared of being duped and taken advantage of. People run the other way if they think we have self-serving, ulterior motives.

True, humble service performed as a follower of Jesus can change the world. It was the Jesus-followers in the Middle Ages who cared for those dying and infected by the Black Plague. And they cleared the streets of dead bodies, either burying or burning them. They had no agenda, but to serve and love. Looking like Jesus is the agenda.

It is not so much about battle lines between what is right and wrong; between the good guys and the bad guys. In fact, I've learned that there really are no good guys and bad guys; there are only bad guys and Jesus. It's Jesus who makes all the difference.

Skye Jethani in his book, *The Great Commodity* tells a story of a point of culture conflict while he was in university.

---

24   Genesis 12:2-3; Galatians 3:7-9

A few months after Skye began his freshman year at Miami University in Oxford, Ohio, the Gay, Lesbian, and Bisexual Alliance (GLBA) sponsored the annual Gay Pride Week on campus with an ensuing "fashion war." It began when the GLBA posted signs announcing "Jean Day." Flyers invited students to show their support for the GLBA's agenda by wearing denim jeans on Thursday. By selecting jeans, it was obvious the GLBA was seeking to inflate their perception of support.

No one really seemed to pay much attention to it until a conservative Christian group began putting up their own signs. Their flyers, distinguishable by a Jesus-fish logo, called students who did not support gay rights to "wear a shirt on Thursday." The battle lines were drawn.

Thursday came, and while most students did not participate in the fashion battle those participating were difficult to miss. Members of the GLBA moved around campus clad in their blue jeans and topless. Some women only wore bras. The conservative Christians marched to class wearing khaki pants and in some cases multiple shirts, proudly doing their part to uphold "righteousness."

It appeared Jean Day would be one of nonviolent self-expression until "Brother Jeb" arrived. Jeb was an itinerant street preacher who came to the campus once or twice a year. He set up his pulpit, a plastic crate, ten yards from the GLBA's "coming-out closet" near the student center. He stood on the crate wearing a placard painted with derogatory words and flames hanging from his shoulders. He shouted through a bull horn promising damnation and calling for repentance.

As a crowd gathered, some laughed at Jeb; others were shocked by his venomous words. A few students could be seen crying. Members of the GLBA arrived on the scene and began arguing with Jeb. As the spectacle kept growing the khaki-wearing Christians were paralyzed. They certainly didn't want to be associated with Brother Jeb, but they couldn't denounce him either. That might be interpreted as supporting the GLBA.

Along comes Dave. Skye explains the confrontation:

> *The mad scene was a microcosm of a culture in which everyone "wears" their identity. The gay community displayed their jeans. The conservatives displayed their khakis. Brother Jeb displayed his flaming placards. There was one exception. Positioned between Jeb's pulpit and the GLBA's closet was Dave. I knew Dave because he lived two floors above me in the dorm, and we became good friends early freshman year. Dave stood amid the chaos in front of the student center with a large metal tank strapped to his back. It was a thermos filled with hot chocolate. With a hose from the backpack he filled cups and offered the free drinks to students on their way to witness the battle between Brother Jeb and the GBLA. Occasionally, someone would stop and ask Dave why he was giving away free drinks. "It's just a way of reminding you that God loves you," he would reply.*

Dave's ministry was not limited to hot chocolate. The morning after a fraternity party he'd enter the house and begin collecting beer cans and cleaning the bathrooms. In the autumn he recruited friends to rake the yards of residents in town. He washed windshields, handed out popsicles on hot days, and even fed parking meters—something campus security did not appreciate given the revenue generated from parking tickets. Dave never accepted a payment or tip of any kind and his goal was not to verbally present the Gospel or leave behind a tract. He simply wanted to show God's love in a tangible way.

This greatly perplexed both the Christians and non-Christians at Miami. When people discovered the motivation behind Dave's service some were uncomfortable. Christians, after all, are prejudiced and belligerent. But how do you disagree with someone who isn't trying to argue? How do you refuse someone's act of kindness who expects nothing in return? The official Christian groups on campus also didn't know what to do with Dave. When he approached them for funds to expand his work they denied his request. Apparently Dave was not doing "real ministry." It did not include signs, posters, flyers, t-shirts, or other forms of legitimate communication, and he refused to display any single Christian ministry's logo. By revealing his identity through loving service Dave was doing more than perplexing the Miami University campus, he was taking his place in a long line of saints who've raised eyebrows by favoring actions over image.[25]

25   Skye Jethani, *The Great Commodity, Zondervan* 2009 pp 59-61

Whenever we choose to actually show God's kindness to those who are not like us and even to those with whom we disagree, we take sides with Jesus.

I've heard a friend of mine pray over and over that not only would God allow him to be the "head and not the tail" (personal blessings), but also "a plus and not a minus." We are either adding value to those around us, we are leaving them as we found them or we are taking from them. Most people are natural takers—minuses—not pluses. Mostly we look for people, places and things to fill our needs. Our example of Jesus is selfless love, adding value wherever it is needed, always being a plus. We're on God's mission, giving time, talent and treasure into others. It is a mission of redemption and transformation.

To do this we must develop a serving strategy—wherever we are. Look for ways to intentionally serve others, using the gifts God has placed in you. Look for the soup kitchen or food pantry meeting the needs of the community. There's probably one there. Volunteer in Jesus' name. No agenda, nothing hidden. No pressure—on you or from you. Don't just give money, but give time and sweat and energy. Serving and seeing; learning and listening.

As Anglican Bishop Tom Wright says:

> *"When the church is seen to move straight from worship of the God we see in Jesus to making a difference and effecting much-needed change in the real world; when it becomes clear that the people who feast at Jesus' table are the ones in the forefront*

of work to eliminate hunger and famine; when people realize that those who pray for the Spirit to work in and through them are the people who seem to have extra resources of love and patience in caring for those whose lives are damaged, bruised, and shamed; then it is not only natural to speak of Jesus himself and to encourage others to worship Him for themselves and find out what belonging to His family is all about but it is also natural for people, however irreligious they may think of themselves as being, to recognize that something is going on that they want to be part of. In terms that the author of Acts might have used, when the church is living out the kingdom of God, the Word of God will spread powerfully and do its own work."[26]

Volunteer at your neighborhood school. Volunteer in the nursing home or the hospice. Serve food at the soup kitchen. Take sandwiches to travelers in the bus station. Be a blessing, like you've been gifted and anointed to be.

WE'VE GOT TO LISTEN

Somewhere in this, we must learn to listen and not talk. When we come only offering solutions without empathy and understanding, we appear inauthentic and uncompassionate. When missionaries cross cultures, they learn to listen to the people around them. If they are smart, they first listen and then talk. They listen to the stories, to the genealogies and to the pain and the passions of the people whose world they have entered.

26 NT Wright, *Surprised by Hope*, (Harper, 2008) p. 267

There are at least three kinds of stories that we tell and to which we listen. Each community and family has them.

Tradition Stories are those stories that connect us with the past and tell us where others have been. When we listen to our community and our neighborhood, we can hear their histories and can feel both the community triumphs and trials. Tradition stories help us know why things are as they are.

But we also need to listen to the community *Vision Stories.* They connect us with the future and tell us where we are going. Everyone has a hope for better things. I have found that everywhere I've been throughout Africa, North America, the Middle East, Russia and Europe people desire a better future for their children than they have for themselves. Whatever the ideology, philosophy or theology everyone wants better for the future and for their offspring than they have today. And if we listen we can hear these stories. They are the dreams of a people.

And perhaps we are best at offering *Map Stories.* As Christ-followers, perhaps we are better able to understand both for ourselves and for the world around us solutions and pathways for change. *Map Stories* help us understand where we are in relationship to both Tradition and Vision and give ideas, rather than dead-bolted solutions. Listening to and telling *Map Stories* offer hope by connecting the right and wrong things in the present with the hope for transformation in the future.

Learning the language, story and customs of the community keeps us from being incomprehensible or irrelevant.

Listening allows us entrance into the world of the people around us. Stories are told from the heart. To share in a story allows vulnerability in both the story-teller and the listener.

Because it is by grace—not our goodness—that we can offer ourselves and our stories to our world without shame. As Believers, our stories are tied to God's purposes. And His purposes are directly tied both to the here-and-now and the future. God's plans and purposes are eternal. He has called, gifted and anointed us to be integral parts of His story of redemption. We see more, we understand more, we are filled with more insight and more compassion and love than others. His grace makes it possible.

We are solutions of hope, wrapped in humility and love. The Spirit is always shaping something bigger than we can imagine - both in us and in our world.

WE'VE GOT TO TELL THE STORY

As we listen to the stories of those around us, we earn the right to tell our story.

Everybody lives a story filled with plot and characters; passion and drama. But as Jesus-followers, we have joined our life stories with God's story. Somehow our subplot has been joined to the cosmic story of salvation, the main plot of a present and active God. We are now part of the whole redemption narrative and God's mission-in-the-earth storyline. And it is an ongoing story, not only about what God did in our lives way back when, but it is the story about what He continues to do in and through our lives. It's a story of hope and fervor. It's a story of faith. Things make sense; we're part of the mission.

Our story is shaped by The Cross. We've been told to take up the cross and follow Jesus into the world, so we are touched by the Cross. We are different. We are different, not just in what we believe about the world, but in how we live in the world.

Some have said, *"Christianity makes no difference because Christians don't believe or practice what they preach."* Sometimes this is a valid complaint. When we espouse something different from what we live, we tell the wrong story. People outside the church know that Jesus was concerned about the poor, the disenfranchised and the sick and are confused when those who claim to follow Jesus are not. We must tell the story of Jesus and the Cross and we must sacrificially live it out in our lives. What we do must reflect what we say. We must live our lives in such a way that they demand an explanation.

Perceptions are as strong as truth. Even wrong perceptions (or maybe *especially* wrong perceptions) are hard to alter, even with the truth. Our perceptions can cause us to act, just as truth can cause us to act, with equal strength. What the world around us thinks of us shapes their thinking and requires us to live intentionally clarifying our beliefs with our actions. The good thing about perceptions is that you can change them. Actions contrary to the established perception can bring them in line with the truth.

We must tell the Cross-shaped story in a way that avoids the "tribal language" of traditional Christianity. It must be told, not as a "we-them" tale expecting them to join up at the end of the story, but as a story of the passion of a loving God. It's about telling the story of Jesus rather than recruiting people for a club. It's about telling a story rather than marketing a program.

We must tell the story to our children and our friends. Wrongly telling the story develops cowards. Telling the right story, in the right way, develops heroes who act on their faith. In the past the Christian story was perceived as being about becoming a good person, a better father or a good and faithful wife or at least escaping hell and going to heaven. In the minds of many, the Gospel was about making us moral and happy and domesticated, making us better citizens and church-attendees. Now the competing stories of our culture are about liberation and freedom, creativity and justice. The stories from our culture sound more like Jesus than the stories the church tells! And this is just wrong.

Somehow, our world has gotten the wrong story. They have bought into a story that does not give the truth about redemption and the joy of following Jesus. It is our responsibility to give the right story about God's love and grace. The mission of God is about redeeming creation, not just sending a select few to eternal bliss. The mission of God is about people living out their reflection of God Himself in character, love, mercy and grace.

The *missio dei* is to redeem men and women so profoundly that they seek justice for others and give mercy liberally, resulting in all creation singing and rejoicing at its arrival!

We need to tell the story and to tell it well; we need to tell it often. We've got to tell the story of Jesus.

WE'VE GOT TO JOURNEY TOGETHER

An African proverb says: *"If you must travel fast, go alone. It you must travel far, go together."* Mission is the long-haul work of the whole church traveling together as "one man" focused on God's plan and mission doing good in the journey. We must honor our diversity—in gifts, personality, perspective, history, heritage—preserving our unity.

We must begin enjoying the journey together, not feeling that the destination is the only thing of value. It is a journey of discovery where we as God's people understand who we are and our part in His mission in the earth. We begin to comprehend something of our usefulness to God because of His gracious investment in us.

We must live together as the Body of Christ with each member having a voice and way to be utilized and finding a place of usefulness in the everyday world of ministry. We are in this together and leadership must equip us to function in our gifts. It is not about being spectators and consumers. It's not about being performers and admirers. It's about all of us, together walking out God's plan.

In living incarnationally (that is embodying Christ in motive, attitude and action) we must establish the church as a counter-culture traveling together in a faith journey. As we honestly honor and love each other, we demonstrate to an on looking world that Jesus is genuine and caring. We must be committed to God's mission in the earth in both evangelism and social justice.

And as we go, we must actually "go!" Being the "sent people of God" means that we actually go and live and do.

AND FINALLY

We can go to the movies, read the books and long for superhero skills. We can fanaticize our way through *Braveheart* or *Lord of the Rings* as their exploits take our breath away. We can settle for being spectators, entertained by big screen adventures wishing the world was a better place. We can attend church and consume sermon after sermon about Bible heroes wishing that what they accomplished we could replicate. We can long for spiritual fulfillment from our places of comfort, secretly knowing that we are created for more.

Or we can realize that God has called us. He really has. He has supernaturally deposited tools in us according to His grand mission. And He wants us involved actively right where we are! He wants us to respond to what He has done both for us and in us.

SO, WHERE DO WE GO FROM HERE?

Live your life from Kingdom perspective, celebrating the unique gifts and calling God has deposited in you! Use the tools invested in you to tell the Story and live out the supernatural Kingdom lifestyle you were created to live!

God can use you! It's His plan.

APPENDIX 1

SPIRITUAL GIFTS AS THE CHURCH GATHERS...

In verse two of 1 Corinthians 12, Paul reminds the Corinthian Believers that in the past they had been led astray by "dumb idols." This is not a value judgment regarding the idols (although that would not seem inappropriate); Paul is referring to idols that did not communicate with the Corinthians. They were mute. They did not speak; there was no communication. They were dumb. But Paul in the context of spiritual gifts is reminding the Corinthian church that they serve a God who communicates with His people. And one of His means of communicating with Believers is through spiritual gifts as they are gathered together.

Paul speaks of diversity of gifts with the same Spirit (12:4). In verse five, he speaks of different administrations but the same Lord. The New American Standard version uses the phrase "differences of ministries," and the Greek word is "diakonia" which refers to "service" or "one who ministers through the executing the command of others." Literally *diakonia* means "through the dust," as one leads and ministers through service. In verse six Paul speaks of "diversities of operations" but the same God. Again, the New American Standard uses the term "varieties of the effects."

And in verse seven, Paul says, "...to each is given the manifestation of the Spirit for the common good." A manifestation of the spirit is something that is seen or heard or experienced.

Even in English the word "manifestation" has an interesting history. Basically "manifestation" means "dancing hand." A manifestation is something that is seen, something that is experienced. In the context of this particular letter, the manifestation of the Spirit happens in the gathering of believers and we see God's Spirit evidence through spiritual gifts. These are occasional gifts. They are given to a specific person on a specific occasion for a specific purpose. They are not resident in the Believer, but are useful to the congregation as a whole as the Spirit apportions to each one individually as He wills.[27] At the gathering of Believers, as is Holy Spirit is working and communicating in the group, the "dancing hand" of spiritual gifts is for the common good.[28]

---

27 1 Corinthians 12:11
28 1 Corinthians 12:7

Now in first Corinthians 12, we can see these supernatural occasional gifts in three groupings:

- _Revelation gifts_ – these give a person the ability to know something by the Holy Spirit that they otherwise would not know.
  - o Word of wisdom
  - o Word of knowledge
  - o Discerning of spirits
- _Power gifts_ – these give a person the ability to do things that they could not do in and of themselves, but can do by the Holy Spirit.
  - o Faith
  - o Gifts of healing
  - o Working of miracles _(dunamis)_
- _Inspiration gifts_ – these give the person the ability to speak and declare things that they would not be able to in and of themselves.
  - o Prophecy
  - o Tongues
  - o Interpretation of tongues

These are all useful for growth in the Body of Christ. And they manifest themselves at the gathering of Believers for the common good. They are there for edification, exhortation and comfort. The insight, knowledge, wisdom and understanding is given as the Spirit sees fit. They are given for the occasion, for the gathering together of Believers, for special insight, information and manifestation of God's power. They are the result of meeting together with a supernatural communicating God and His people.

They are tools not toys. And very powerful tools at that! In the early church, they were not considered accessories, but necessities. In meeting together, God was in their midst with instructions and encouragement and power for their everyday lives.

And yet we must emphasize that these were gifts of grace; they were not earned, but were given according to whomever God chose and however He chooses. And that's what grace is all about, isn't it?

APPENDIX 2

LISTING OF GIFTS

	Eph 4: 11-12	Rom 12: 6-8	1CO 12: 8-10
List of Gifts	Apostles Prophets Evangelists Pastors Teachers	Prophecy Serving Teaching Exhorting Giving Leading Showing Mercy	Word of Wisdom Word of Knowledge Faith Gifts of Healing Miracles Prophecy Discerning of Spirits Kinds of tongues Interpretation of tongues
Number of Gifts	5	7	9
The Giver	Christ	God	Holy Spirit
Type of Gifts and Related Greek Word	Gifts of Christ Domata (v.8)	Gifts of God's Grace Charismata (v.6)	Gifts of the Holy Spirit Pneumatikos (v.1)
Description	Equipping Gifts	Functional Gifts	Manifestation Gifts
Related Passages	1CO 12:27-30	1Pe 4:10,11; 1TI 4:14; 2TI 1:6	Rom 1:11; 1 CO 12:27-30.

Made in the
USA
Middletown, DE